STAR WARS

ATTACK ON READING

COMING ATTRACTIONS....

Chewbacca in the Death Star

X-wing fighters

Artoo saves the day.

STARRING....

Luke Skywalker A young farmer who lives on the planet Tatooine.

Artoo Detoo (R2-D2) A clever, computer type of robot.

Han Solo Captain of the *Millennium Falcon*, a Corellian starship.

Grand Moff Tarkin An Imperial Governor.

See Threepio (C-3PO) A tall, humanlike robot who translates all kinds of languages.

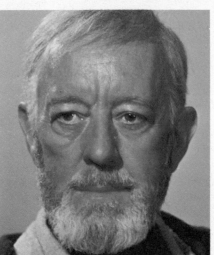

Ben (Obi-wan) Kenobi A good and just warrior of the Old Republic who possesses a special power called the Force.

Darth Vader The evil Imperial Dark Lord who tries to crush the Rebellion.

Chewbacca A two-hundred-year-old "Wookiee" whose language is only grunts and growls.

Princess Leia Organa A young Senator who is secretly leading the Rebellion against the evil Imperial forces.

Death Star A gigantic and powerful satellite battle station built by Governor Tarkin.

Hello! I am See Threepio. You say it like this: C-3PO. My little round friend here is Artoo Detoo. You say it like this: R2D2. We are both "droids," or robots.

Artoo works with computers. When a person needs to know something, Artoo plugs himself into a computer to find the answer. Since he speaks only the language of computers, I will speak for him.

Artoo and I will help you read the story of STAR WARS. Before you read each part of the story you will learn some words that you may not know. The words and their meanings will be in a WORD COMPUTER. Each word is followed by its pronunciation. Here is an example: **Rebel** (reb′el) - person fighting against the Galactic Empire.

To find out how to pronounce a word in the WORD COMPUTER, you can look at the Pronunciation Key below.

PRONUNCIATION KEY

act, āble, dâre, ärt

ebb, ēqual

if, īce

hot, ōver, ôrder

oil

book

ooze

out

up, ûrge

ə = a as in alone

ə as in button (bu′tən), fire (fīər)

chief

shoe

thin

that

zh as in measure (mezh′ ər)

The symbol (′) as in (muth′ ər) is used to show primary, or heavy, stress. The symbol (′) as in (grand′ muth′ ər), is used to show secondary or lighter, stress.

This is a summary of the first half of the STAR WARS story in Comprehension 1.

Along time ago, in a galaxy far, far away, a great adventure took place . . . .

Luke Skywalker lived on a farm with his aunt and uncle on the far-off planet of Tatooine. Luke was bored with life on the farm and longed for adventure and excitement.

In another part of the galaxy, a great war was taking place between a small Rebel army and the evil Imperial forces. The Rebels were greatly outnumbered, yet they fought bravely on.

One of the Rebel leaders, Princess Leia Organa, captured the secret plans to the Death Star, a powerful Imperial battle station. The Rebels hoped to use these plans to defeat the Empire.

In a deadly battle high above Tatooine, Princess Leia was captured by the evil Imperial leader, Darth Vader. She had already hidden the plans and a message for Obi-wan Kenobi, who had fought against the Empire long ago, in a small droid named Artoo Detoo. Artoo's mission was to deliver the plans to the Rebels.

While the battle raged, Artoo and his fellow droid, See Threepio, escaped to Tatooine. There they were captured and sold to Luke's aunt and uncle. Artoo, trying to complete his mission, escaped from the farm one night. The next day, Luke and Threepio set out to track him down. After they had found him, they were attacked by sandpeople, and were rescued by Obi-wan Kenobi. After hearing Artoo's message, Kenobi asked Luke to join him in fighting the Empire. Luke refused and returned alone to the farm.

While Luke and Threepio had been searching for Artoo, Imperial stormtroopers had come to the farm, burned it down and killed Luke's aunt and uncle. Seeing this destruction, Luke decided to join Kenobi. Together they were determined to deliver Artoo and the plans to the Rebels.

Now read the exciting conclusion of the story of STAR WARS.

DETAILS

Hello there! Artoo and I are glad to see you. You have seen us in a space battle, lost on the Tatooine desert, captured by those horrid little jawas, and attacked by sandpeople.

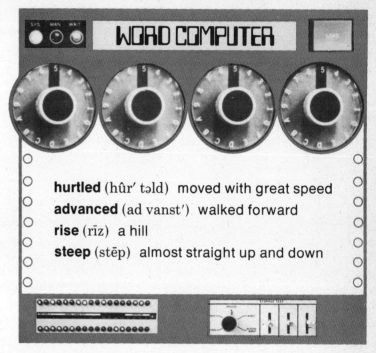

WORD COMPUTER

hurtled (hûr′ təld) moved with great speed
advanced (ad vanst′) walked forward
rise (rīz) a hill
steep (stēp) almost straight up and down

TAKEOFF

DETAILS are the FACTS that make up a story. Reading DETAILS will help you understand what is happening in the story. (DETAILS, or FACTS, form the skeleton of a story.)

MISSION

Complete questions 1 through 4 by circling the letter of the choice that best answers each question. Complete questions 5 and 6 by writing the answer to each in the space provided.

1. Who broke the silence in the landspeeder?
   a. Luke
   b. Artoo
   c. Kenobi
   d. Threepio

2. What had the stormtroopers done to change Luke's life?
   a. stolen his droids
   b. killed his aunt and uncle
   c. killed his father
   d. built the Death Star

3. How long did it take for the stormtroopers to destroy the farm?
   a. a day
   b. twenty years
   c. a month
   d. a few minutes

4. What does Luke want to learn from Kenobi?
   a. about Kenobi's life
   b. about Alderaan
   c. about the Force
   d. about the landspeeder

5. Where did Kenobi want Luke to stop his landspeeder?

   _____

6. Where had Luke chosen to go with Kenobi?

   _____

Luke did not know what his future would bring. All he knew was that his old life was finished forever. Uncle Owen, Aunt Beru, and the farm where he had lived his whole life were gone.

In only a few moments, the evil stormtroopers of the Galactic Empire had wiped out all Luke had ever known and loved.

Luke turned to Obi-wan Kenobi. "I want to come with you to Alderaan," Luke said. "There's nothing here for me now. I want to learn the ways of the Force and become a Jedi like my father."

Kenobi nodded, then placed his arm about the young man's shoulder. The two walked slowly toward the parked landspeeder. The old man was talking quietly to Luke. Luke did not speak, he only listened.

When the two neared the landspeeder, Luke called out to the droids. "Threepio! Artoo! Hurry up. Get into the speeder. We're heading for Mos Eisley spaceport."

The four travelers climbed into Luke's speeder. Luke started the engine and the speeder leaped forward. Soon, they were traveling rapidly over the hot sands of the Tatooine desert.

Luke and Kenobi prepare to leave.

As the speeder hurtled toward Mos Eisley, Luke and Obi-wan rode in silence. Each was lost in his own thoughts of the future. In time, the land grew rocky and began to rise.

It was Kenobi who broke the silence. "Head toward that hill over there," he said. "Then stop."

Luke turned the speeder toward the tall, rocky rise that Kenobi had pointed out. When the speeder came to a halt, Luke, Kenobi, and the two droids got out. Following Obi-wan, the others advanced toward the edge of a steep cliff.

"What is it?" asked Luke. "What's over there?"

"You'll see in a minute," Obi-wan answered. "There's something I want to show you."

DETAILS

Just thinking about the details, or facts, brings oil to my brow. How can you take it so calmly, Artoo? Have you no feelings? What's that? I know, Artoo, your whole life is built around storing and giving details.

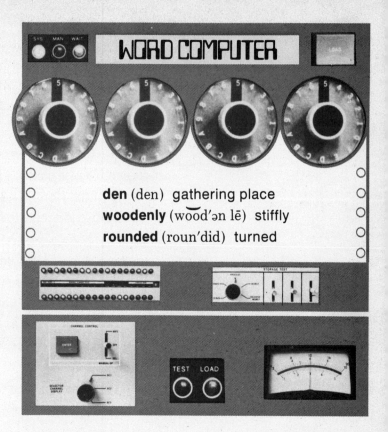

WORD COMPUTER

den (den) gathering place
woodenly (woŏd'ən lē) stiffly
rounded (roun'did) turned

FLIGHT PLAN

DETAILS can help you find answers to FACT questions. A DETAIL will answer the questions WHO? WHAT? WHERE? and WHEN? Check to see that the answer to each type of question is a FACT stated in the story.

MISSION

Complete questions 1 through 4 by circling the letter of the choice that best completes each sentence. Complete questions 5 and 6 by writing the answer to each in the space provided.

1. The streets of the city were ____.
   a. crowded and wide
   b. empty and wide
   c. narrow and crowded
   d. narrow and empty

2. The name of the city is ____.
   a. Tosche Space Station
   b. Alderaan
   c. Tatooine
   d. Mos Eisley

3. The speeder was surrounded by ____.
   a. stormtroopers
   b. a dust storm
   c. sandpeople
   d. Rebel troops

4. The stormtroopers demanded to see Luke's ____.
   a. parents
   b. papers
   c. school records
   d. landspeeder

5. Each stormtrooper carried ____.

   _____

6. Luke told the stormtroopers he had owned the droids for about ____.

   _____

   _____

Obi-wan waved Luke and the two droids forward. They went to the edge of the cliff and looked down. A city lay spread out in the valley below.

Kenobi said, "Take a good look, Luke. There's Mos Eisley spaceport. You'll not find an uglier den of evil people anywhere in the galaxy. We must be careful. I'm sure the Empire has sent word out to find our droids. It will be dangerous in Mos Eisley, but we have a great deal to do there. Let's get moving."

Luke drove the speeder and his three passengers down into the city. The streets of Mos Eisley were narrow and crowded. Creatures from every corner of the galaxy walked the narrow streets.

As Luke rounded a corner, he was forced to bring the speeder to a quick halt. Several stormtroopers in white armor surrounded Luke and his friends. Each trooper carried a deadly laser rifle.

The lead trooper looked closely at the two droids in the speeder. "How long have you had these droids?" he asked Luke.

"About three or four seasons," Luke answered.

"Let me see your papers," the trooper demanded of Luke.

Luke nervously began to search his pockets for the papers he knew he didn't have.

Kenobi stared into the trooper's eyes and spoke to him in a low, direct voice. "You don't need to see his papers. These are not the droids you're looking for. We can go about our business."

The trooper turned to the other soldiers. He spoke woodenly to them. "We don't need to see his papers. These are not the droids we're looking for. They can go about their business."

Luke did not know what happened or how Kenobi had done it, but he did not wait to find out. He gunned the speeder ahead. "What strange power had Kenobi used?" Luke thought to himself.

Stormtroopers surround the landspeeder.

SOLO ● Do this part of the lesson on your own. Follow the steps that you used in the other parts of this lesson. May the Force be with you!

WORD COMPUTER

crumbled (krum′bəld) broken down
stream (strēm) a steady flow
cantina (kan tē′nə) a saloon, much like that found in the American Old West

MISSION Complete questions 1 through 4 by circling the letter of the choice that best answers each question. Complete questions 5 and 6 by writing the answer to each in the space provided.

1. In what part of town was the cantina located?
   a. the outskirts
   b. the best
   c. the oldest
   d. the newest

2. What happened to the streets as Luke drove deeper into the city?
   a. They got cleaner.
   b. They got narrower.
   c. They became safer.
   d. They became more curved.

3. What kinds of humans and creatures were in the cantina?
   a. quiet and lonely
   b. friendly and happy
   c. big and mean
   d. mean and rough

4. Who gathered around Luke's speeder to look it over?
   a. jawas
   b. stormtroopers
   c. unknown creatures
   d. Rebels

5. What two noises filled the cantina?

   _____

   _____

6. On whom does the Force have a strange effect?

   _____

   _____

Kenobi directed Luke through the streets of the city. It appeared that Kenobi had been there before. He knew exactly where he was headed.

Luke was interested in everything around him. He had never seen so many strange creatures in one place at one time. The deeper Luke drove into the city, the narrower the streets became.

In a few minutes, Kenobi asked Luke to stop the speeder. By the looks of the neighborhood this had to be the oldest part of the city. Luke looked at the dirty streets and crumbled buildings.

Obi-wan's voice broke into Luke's thoughts. "It's over there, Luke," he said. "That's what we're looking for. It's that old cantina." The old man was pointing to a dirty old building that housed a saloon.

Luke saw a stream of mean, rough-looking humans and creatures pass through the cantina's doors. The noises of laughter and fighting filled the air.

Luke parked the speeder and climbed out. Obi-wan and the two droids also got out. From nowhere, several jawas gathered to look at the speeder. They chattered excitedly until Luke chased them away.

Luke walked with Kenobi toward the cantina. Threepio and Artoo followed a short distance behind. Luke was speaking to Obi-wan. "I thought we were dead back there. What happened?"

"It was the Force," Kenobi said. "A great deal of the Force is in the mind, Luke. The Force can have a strange effect on the weak-minded."

Luke did not fully understand what Kenobi meant. He began to speak about something else. "Do you really think we're going to find a pilot to take us to Alderaan?" Luke asked.

"Well, most of the best freighter pilots can be found here," Kenobi said. "Only watch your step. This place can be a little rough."

"I'm ready for anything," Luke said.

"Come along, Artoo," Threepio added.

The two humans and their droid friends entered the smoke-filled cantina.

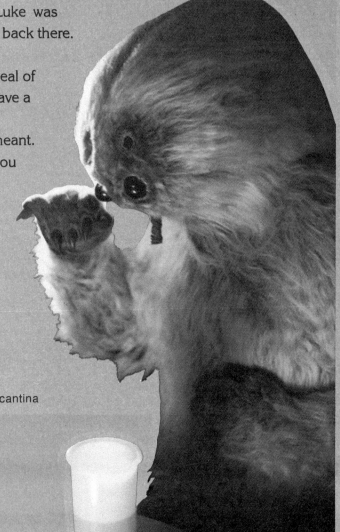

a guest in the cantina

MAIN IDEA/TITLE

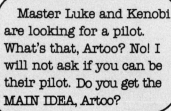

Master Luke and Kenobi are looking for a pilot. What's that, Artoo? No! I will not ask if you can be their pilot. Do you get the MAIN IDEA, Artoo?

WORD COMPUTER

accustomed (ə kus′təmd) used (to)
spun (spun) turned quickly
responded (ri spon′ did) answered

TAKEOFF

The MAIN IDEA of a story tells about the ENTIRE story. A MAIN IDEA tells the idea in the story in just one sentence. The MAIN IDEA is the most important idea in the story.

MISSION

Circle the letter of the choice that best completes each statement. For questions 5 and 6 write your own answers.

1. The main idea of the story is the cantina _____.
   a. was dark
   b. was in Mos Eisley
   c. was a strange place
   d. was crowded

2. Luke was spun around roughly by the _____.
   a. waiter
   b. Wookiee
   c. cantina door
   d. droids

3. Luke wanted a cool drink of _____
   a. soda pop
   b. milk
   c. water
   d. juice

4. Luke asked Artoo and Threepio to _____.
   a. wait outside
   b. look for Kenobi
   c. look for a pilot
   d. buy him dinner

5. The Wookiee had _____

   eyes and a rather _____
   smile.

6. Some of the creatures in the cantina were

   _____-eyed, some were

   _____-eyed, and some had

   _____ eyes.

12

It was dark in the cantina. At first, Luke could see nothing. In a few minutes, when his eyes became accustomed to the dark, he saw something which shocked him. The cantina was filled with creatures. There were one-eyed creatures, thousand-eyed creatures, and creatures with no eyes. Some had skin that moved in waves. Others had fur. Luke could not remember ever seeing a group as odd as this.

Luke turned to Kenobi. "I thought we were looking for a pilot."

"So we are, young Luke, so we are," Kenobi responded. Kenobi pushed forward through the crowded cantina. Luke followed. Luke had not gone far when a hand grabbed his shirt and roughly spun him around. Luke turned to see the ugly face of a waiter.

"We don't allow droids here!" the waiter said, pointing angrily over Luke's shoulder. "They'll have to wait outside. We don't want droids in here. This is a nice place."

Luke spoke to Threepio. It was no time to look for trouble. "Listen," Luke said, "why don't you and Artoo wait outside by the speeder. We'll be out in a while anyhow. I need a cool drink of soda pop."

inside the cantina

"I fully agree with you, sir," Threepio said even before Luke had finished. "Come along, Artoo," the tall golden droid said to his little pal. "We're well rid of this place!" Then the two droids pushed through the doors of the cantina. In an instant, they were gone.

Luke turned back to the bar. He spotted Kenobi. He was talking to a creature Luke had often heard about, but had never seen. It was a Wookiee. The towering Wookiee stood over seven feet tall. From head to toe it was covered with thick, reddish-brown hair. The huge monkeylike creature had a surprisingly pleasant face, bright yellow eyes, and a rather toothy smile.

Kenobi was talking to the Wookiee in its own language. Once again, the old man had shown Luke that there was more to him than met the eye.

★ 2 MAIN IDEA/TITLE

Hurry up, Artoo. This story reminds me of a movie I saw just the other day. I can't remember its TITLE. What, Artoo? Oh. A TITLE is a word or phrase we use to name something like a story.

WORD COMPUTER

shoved (shuvd) pushed roughly
boasted (bōs′ təd) bragged
described (di skrībd′) told about in words or pictures

FLIGHT PLAN

The TITLE, or name, of a story should also tell its MAIN IDEA. Remember that the MAIN IDEA is the most important idea in the whole story. A TITLE usually tells you what the story is going to be about.

MISSION

For questions 1 to 4, circle the letter of the choice that best answers each question. For questions 5 and 6, write your own answers in the space provided.

1. What is the best title for this part of the story?
   a. The Creatures
   b. The Cantina
   c. Luke in Danger
   d. Luke's Heart

2. Where did the almost-human creature push his finger?
   a. into the many-eyed creature
   b. into Luke's glass
   c. into the Wookiee
   d. into Luke's chest

3. What was Luke's last thought?
   a. ''I'll be careful.''
   b. ''My life is over.''
   c. ''Where is Ben?''
   d. ''Will we get to Alderaan?''

4. In how many galaxies did the monster have the death penalty?
   a. twelve
   b. many
   c. none
   d. twenty

5. What is another good title for this part of the story?

   _____

   _____

6. What did the monster point at Luke's chest?

   _____

Before Luke could get his drink, he was shoved roughly into the cantina. Luke turned in anger. He was fully ready to fight. Whoever had pushed him was going to pay for it.

What Luke saw facing him stopped him dead in his tracks. It was a large, many-eyed creature. Its body was so ugly it could not even be described. Standing next to the many-eyed creature was an almost-human form. The almost-human pushed its finger roughly into Luke's chest.

"He doesn't like you," the almost-human monster said to Luke.

"I'm sorry," Luke said to the many-eyed creature, then turned away.

"I don't like you either," the monster said. "You just watch yourself. We're wanted men. I have the death sentence in twelve galaxies," the monster boasted.

"I'll be careful then," Luke said, not knowing what else to say.

"Careful!" the monster shouted. "You'll be dead!" With that, he reached into his shirt and pulled out a deadly laser pistol.

All the other creatures in the cantina moved quietly away from Luke. It was clear to them that there was going to be trouble.

Before Luke knew it, he was standing alone facing a crazed monster who wanted to kill him.

The monster came toward Luke. The young farmer was frozen with fear. What could he do against the armed monster?

"My life is over," Luke thought.

With each second the monster came closer. His weapon was now pointed at Luke's heart.

Luke meets the creature.

SOLO

● Do this part of the lesson on your own. Follow the steps that you used in the other parts of this lesson. May the Force be with you!

WORD COMPUTER

slipped (slipd) moved quietly
accept (ak sep′t) to take
severed (sev′ərd) cut off

MISSION

For questions 1 to 4, circle the letter of the choice that best completes each statement. For questions 5 and 6, write your answers to complete the sentences.

1. The main idea of this part of the story is that _____.
   a. Kenobi fought to save Luke's life
   b. Kenobi killed a monster
   c. the waiter tried to stop the fight
   d. Kenobi had a lightsaber

2. Kenobi kept his weapon in his _____.
   a. speeder
   b. boot
   c. belt
   d. shirt

3. When the fighting was over, _____.
   a. Luke was badly injured
   b. the customers were silent
   c. Kenobi bought dinner
   d. the band began to play

4. The beam of Kenobi's lightsaber was _____.
   a. red
   b. invisible
   c. blue-white
   d. silent

5. A title for this part of the story might be _____.

   _____

   _____

6. It took Kenobi only a _____ to draw his lightsaber from his belt.

   _____

Luke did not know it, but Kenobi had slipped silently in behind him. Kenobi spoke calmly to the monster. "This little one's not worth the trouble," the old man said. "Come let me buy you a drink."

The monster did not accept Kenobi's offer. Instead, he lashed out with his huge arm. The blow struck Luke across the face. He went spinning across the room, crashing into several tables.

The monster let out a loud scream. From his belt the monster pulled a second laser pistol, even bigger than the first. In a flash both lasers pointed at Kenobi.

The waiter's voice cut through the air. "No blasters! No blasters!" he yelled. "Not in here!"

The monster turned toward the waiter to silence him.

It was all the time Kenobi needed. In a split-second, the old man's hand moved to his belt. A bright, blue-white beam seemed to grow from his hand. A strange humming noise filled the cantina.

The blue-white beam of Kenobi's lightsaber swept up and over the monster. A horrible scream came from the monster's lips as he fell against the bar. Before he died, he stared at the floor. His severed arm lay on the floor.

Kenobi carefully turned off the beam of his lightsaber. He replaced the weapon in his belt. The monster was dragged away. In a few moments, all was normal in the cantina. The band began to play.

Kenobi kills the monster.

MAIN IDEA/DETAILS

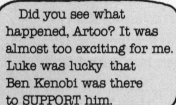

Did you see what happened, Artoo? It was almost too exciting for me. Luke was lucky that Ben Kenobi was there to SUPPORT him.

WORD COMPUTER

○ **first mate** (fûrst māt) second in command to the captain of a ship
○ **Millennium Falcon** (mi len'ē əm   fal kən) the name of a spacecraft owned by Captain Han Solo
○ **skill** (skil) an unusual ability or art

TAKEOFF

The MAIN IDEA tells the reader the most important idea in the story. A MAIN IDEA is explained, or proven, by some of the DETAILS of the story. These are called SUPPORTING DETAILS. A good reader will be able to use the SUPPORTING DETAILS to prove the MAIN IDEA.

MISSION

For questions 1 and 2, circle the letter of the choice that best answers each question about the story. (In the second question you will circle more than one letter.) For questions 3 and 4, write your answers in the space.

1. What is the main idea of the story?
   a. Chewbacca is a giant Wookiee.
   b. There is much talk of the fight.
   c. Kenobi and Solo wish to make a deal.
   d. Luke is lucky to be alive.

2. Which 4 details support the main idea?
   a. The ship is the Millenium Falcon.
   b. Chewie told Solo of Kenobi's wish to reach Alderaan.
   c. Kenobi thinks Solo's ship meets their need.
   d. Luke felt safe in the cantina.
   e. Kenobi wished to get on with his business.

   f. Solo praised Kenobi's saberplay.
   g. Kenobi wants to meet the ship's captain.

3. What is a good title for this part of the story?

   _____

   _____

4. Where was Han Solo seated?

   _____

Luke thought about his near brush with death. He was shaken by the speed with which the fight had ended and the power of Kenobi's lightsaber. Kenobi was unlike anyone Luke had ever known.

Luke and Kenobi stood at the bar. All about them the talk was of the fight that had just taken place.

"Are you all right?" Kenobi asked Luke. "You had a close call."

"I'm okay," Luke answered. "I'm just lucky you were there. If . . ."

Kenobi placed his arm around the young man's shoulders. "Enough of that," Kenobi said. "Let's get on with our business."

"This is Chewbacca," Kenobi said, pointing to the giant Wookiee. "He is first mate on a ship that may meet our needs. He'll take us to the captain now."

Kenobi and Luke followed Chewbacca to the rear of the cantina. For the first time since he entered the cantina, Luke felt safe. "Who," he thought, "would be foolish enough to attack me in the company of a Jedi and the seven-foot Wookiee?"

They neared a table that stood in the cantina's darkest corner. A handsome young man was seated at the table. Or **was** he a young man? It was hard to tell. The captain waved Kenobi and Luke into seats. Chewbacca lowered himself into the other chair.

"That was nice saberplay, Kenobi," said the young man. "It's not often one sees such skill in this part of the Empire."

The man held out his hand to Kenobi. "Glad to meet you," he said. "I'm Han Solo. I'm captain of the Millennium Falcon."

Kenobi nodded his greetings to the captain. Solo pointedly looked away from Luke. It was clear to the captain who was in charge here.

"Chewie here tells me you're looking for passage to the Alderaan system," Solo said. "Perhaps we can get together," he added with a smile.

Kenobi returned Solo's smile. "Perhaps," he said. "Perhaps."

Han Solo

Artoo, try not to get so excited. We droids must remain calm at all times. What's that? You want to know if I have any FACTS to SUPPORT my idea. I mean really, Artoo, after all our time together you should SUPPORT me!

WORD COMPUTER

cargo (kär′ gō) something carried aboard a ship for trade or fee

parsecs (pär′ seks) units of time, similar to seconds

steer clear of (stēr′ klēr′ uv′) stay away from

FLIGHT PLAN

As you read, think about the DETAILS that SUPPORT the MAIN IDEA of the story. The SUPPORTING DETAILS explain the MAIN IDEA more fully. SUPPORTING DETAILS can often tell you what is being described. They also make a story interesting to read!

MISSION

For questions 1 and 3, write your answers in the space provided. For question two, circle the letter of each of the 5 details that support the main idea.

1. What is the main idea of this part of the story?

    _____

    _____

2. Which details support the main idea?
    a. The ship will leave when Kenobi is ready.
    b. The ship is a fast ship.
    c. Luke is a good pilot.
    d. Solo quickly accepted the offer.
    e. Solo thought Kenobi had insulted him.
    f. Solo will be paid seventeen thousand dollars.
    g. Imperial stormtroopers are in the cantina.

    h. Solo said to meet him at Docking Bay 94.
    i. Kenobi will pay Solo two thousand now and fifteen thousand later.

3. What would be a good title for this part of the story?

    _____

    _____

4. How much will Kenobi pay Solo to fly to Alderaan?

    _____

    _____

Solo looked puzzled. "What do you mean?" he asked Kenobi. "Do you want to get to Alderaan or not?"

"Yes, indeed," answered Kenobi. "If it's a fast ship you've got."

Solo looked hurt. "A fast ship?" he asked. "A fast ship? You've never heard of the Millennium Falcon?" Solo asked with wonder in his voice.

Kenobi looked amused. "Should I have?"

"It's the ship that made the Kessel run in less than twelve parsecs," he replied angrily. "I've outrun Imperial starships. Not the local cruisers, but the big Corellian ships. I think it's fast enough for you. What's the cargo?"

Kenobi glanced about the cantina before he answered. No one seemed to be listening. "Only passengers," he said quietly. "Myself, the boy, two droids — and no questions asked. We would also like to steer clear of meeting any Imperial warships."

Solo smiled. "Well that's the whole trick, isn't it? And it's going to cost you ten thousand."

"Ten thousand!" Luke said excitedly. "We could almost buy our own ship for that!"

Luke, Kenobi, and Solo

"But who's going to fly it, kid?" Solo asked. "You?"

It was Luke's turn to look insulted. "You bet I could," he said. "I'm not such a bad pilot myself. We don't have to sit here and listen . . ."

Kenobi looked at Solo. "We can pay you two thousand now plus fifteen when we reach Alderaan."

Solo did not have to think very long about the offer. "Seventeen!" he said. "You guys just bought yourselves a ship. We'll leave as soon as you're ready. Meet Chewie and me at Docking Bay 94. You'd better hurry up. It looks like those Imperial stormtroopers are interested in your lightsaber act, Kenobi. Mightly interested."

SOLO

● Do this part of the lesson on your own. Follow the steps that you used in the other parts of this lesson. May The Force Be With You!

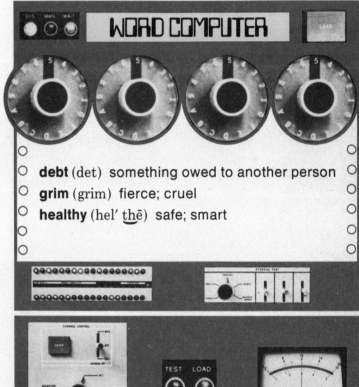

WORD COMPUTER

debt (det) something owed to another person
grim (grim) fierce; cruel
healthy (hel' thē) safe; smart

MISSION

Complete each statement by writing your own answer in the space provided. Write complete sentences whenever possible.

1. What is the main idea of this part of the story?

_____

_____

2. What are 5 details that support the main idea?

a. _____

b. _____

c. _____

d. _____

e. _____

3. What would be a good title for this part of the story?

_____

_____

4. To whom does Han Solo owe money?

_____

Luke and Ben slipped quietly out of the cantina. When they had gone, Solo spoke to Chewbacca. "Seventeen thousand! Those two must really be in trouble. This could really save my neck. Get back to the ship, Chewie, and get her ready."

Chewie left quickly. Solo leaned back in his chair. With the money he could finally pay off all the money he owed to Jabba. It wasn't healthy to owe money to Jabba. If Solo didn't pay him soon, it could be dangerous. Jabba was not one to forget a debt. Han pushed his chair from the table. He stood up to leave the cantina.

Before he stood fully, a long green arm pushed him roughly back into his chair. "Going somewhere, Solo?" an electronic voice asked.

Solo looked up in surprise. A deadly laser pistol was pointed at his face.

Solo remained calm. "Yes, Greedo, as a matter of fact, I was just going to see your boss. Tell Jabba that I've got his money."

Greedo gave a grim smile. "It's too late. You should have paid him a long time ago. Jabba has put a price on your head. The reward is so large every hunter in the galaxy will be looking for you. I'm lucky I found you first."

"Wait a minute!" Solo said. "I have the money."

Greedo smiled again. "If you give me the money, I might forget I found you." he said. "I can't wait very long, Solo. Jabba will surely take your ship."

Han talks business with Greedo.

"Over my dead body," Solo replied. Beneath the table, Han had quietly drawn his laser pistol.

"That's not a bad idea," said Greedo. "I've been looking forward to killing you for a long time, Solo. Let's go outside. We . . ."

Greedo never said another word. His ugly green body seemed to explode in the seat. Smoke and white-hot light covered the chair where Greedo had sat.

For a moment all heads turned toward Solo and the still-smoking Greedo. Solo stood up and walked quickly out of the cantina.

23

We just "scraped through" that part of the story. What do I mean by "scrape through?" In this case it means "to get through something dangerous."

WORD COMPUTER

dared (dârd) had the courage to

fuss (fus) a great deal of trouble

TAKEOFF

Sometimes you find a word in a sentence that has two or more possible meanings. A good way to find the proper meaning is to look at the whole sentence. Decide which meaning will make the most sense in the sentence. As you read the story on the next page, pay special attention to the underlined words.

MISSION

For questions 1 to 4, circle the letter of the choice that best tells the meaning of each word as it is used in the story. For questions 5 and 6, write your own answers.

1. The word "lurked" means _____.
   a. started   c. hid
   b. fought   d. wet

2. The word "clad" means _____.
   a. happy   c. faced
   b. dressed   d. washed

3. The word "dispatched" means _____.
   a. torn   c. shot
   b. presented   d. sent

4. The word "peered" means _____.
   a. looked secretly c. peeled
   b. selected   d. climbed

5. The word "crack" means _____.

   _____

   Another meaning for "crack" is _____.

   _____

6. The word "watch" means _____.

   _____

   Another meaning for "watch" is _____.

   _____

Armed stormtroopers hurried down the street. The stormtroopers, clad in white armor, moved through the narrow streets at will. No one dared block their path. No one questioned them. They were soldiers of the Galactic Empire.

One trooper left the group. His leader had dispatched him to check the doors of the houses that lined the street.

"Those missing droids could be here," he thought. The several doors he tried were closed and locked.

"Hurry up," the trooper's leader called out. "Those droids are probably far from Mos Eisley by now."

"The doors are locked anyway," the trooper called. He ran after the other soldiers, who were already turning the corner.

The instant the troopers were out of sight, one of the doors opened a crack. A golden metal face peered carefully out. "It seems to be clear," Threepio said to Artoo.

"I would rather have gone with Master Luke than stay here with you. I don't know what all this fuss is about. But I'm sure it must be your fault."

Artoo chirped a series of nasty-sounding whistles and beeps.

Threepio looked angrily down at the little droid. "You watch your language!" Threepio warned. "You'd better watch yourself. Here comes Luke now."

A strange figure lurked in the shadows of a hidden doorway. It watched the approaching Luke and Kenobi with great interest. Who could this strange figure be? What did he want with Luke and Kenobi?

Stormtroopers chase the droids.

VOCABULARY

Artoo, keep an eye on that fellow watching Ben and Luke. He is certainly up to no good. I would bet, if I were a betting droid, that he works for the Empire. One never knows whom to trust these days. No, no, Artoo! I trust **you.**

WORD COMPUTER

- **cloak** (klōk) a loose-fitting piece of clothing.
- **arrival** (ə rī′vəl) coming to a destination
- **rarely** (râr′ lē) not often
- **uneven** (un ē′ vən) rough; not smooth
- **foursome** (fōr′ səm) a group of four

FLIGHT PLAN

After you read the story on the next page, go back and read each sentence with an underlined word. Decide which meaning would make the most sense in the sentence. Remember, think about the meaning of the word as it is used in the story. Learning to figure out the meaning of a new word will help you understand the story.

MISSION

For questions 1 to 4, circle the letter of the choice that best tells the meaning of each word as it is used in the story. For questions 5 and 6, write your own answers.

1. The word "noted" means _____.
   a. said
   b. famous
   c. saw
   d. split

2. The word "pace" means _____.
   a. steps
   b. put in a bag
   c. without fighting
   d. measure

3. The word "seeking" means _____.
   a. being caught
   b. looking for
   c. parties
   d. kneeling

4. The word "tongue" means _____.
   a. feeling
   b. causing
   c. mouth part
   d. language

5. The word "energy" means _____.

   _____

   Write a sentence using the word "energy."

   _____

6. The word "boasts" means _____.

   _____

   Write a sentence using the word "boasts."

   _____

The stranger dressed in dark clothing <u>noted</u> the arrival of Kenobi and Luke. "Could these be the two travelers the stormtroopers were <u>seeking</u>? If so, where were the two droids that were supposed to be with them?" the stranger thought.

Just then, Threepio and Artoo left the doorway in which they were hiding. Kenobi, Luke, Threepio and Artoo stood together for a moment. They seemed to be talking.

"It had to be them!," the stranger thought. From beneath his cloak the stranger took a small but powerful radio. Lifting the radio to what must have been his mouth, the stranger spoke quietly into the radio. He spoke in a strange <u>tongue</u> one rarely heard on Tatooine.

The foursome walked quickly away. They headed for Docking Bay 94. The group moved with the sure steps of those who knew where they were going. The stranger followed at a safe distance.

Surprisingly, Luke had to quicken his <u>pace</u> to keep up with Kenobi. The old man seemed to be growing stronger and steadier with each passing moment. It was as if the Force were alive within him, giving him new <u>energy</u>.

"I hated to sell my speeder so cheaply," Luke said, holding out a handful of small coins to Kenobi.

Kenobi gave Luke a kindly smile. "That will be enough. I've got some money of my own to add to yours. Besides if the ship is as fast as Solo <u>boasts</u> it is, we'll be okay."

A loud chattering noise caught their attention. The furry head of Chewbacca stood out above the crowd in the street. He was waving his arms as a signal to follow him.

"I wonder what he's so excited about?" Luke asked Kenobi.

"We'll soon know. There's Docking Bay 94 now," Kenobi said, pointing toward a large uneven hole cut into the ground.

Luke sells his landspeeder.

★ VOCABULARY

SOLO
● Do this part of the lesson on your own. Follow the steps that you used in the other parts of the lesson. May the Force be with you!

WORD COMPUTER

spare (spâr) left over, extra
panel (pan'əl) a board with instruments or controls
counts (kounts) is important

MISSION
For questions 1 to 4, circle the letter of the choice that best tells the meaning of the word as it is used in the story. For questions 5 and 6, write your own answers.

1. The word "fashioned" means ____.
   a. modern   c. made of
   b. clothing   d. a method

2. The word "grand" means ____.
   a. large   c. ugly
   b. one thousand   d. fancy

3. The word "gouged" means ____.
   a. opened   c. measured
   b. dug   d. piled

4. The word "battered" means ____.
   a. beaten and dented   c. small and tough
   b. soft and loose   d. large and shiny

5. The word "minute" means ____.

   _____

   Write a sentence using the word "minute."

   _____

6. The word "enormous" means ____.

   _____

   Write a sentence using the word "enormous."

   _____

28

Docking Bay 94 was not as <u>grand</u> as its name. It was no more than a simple stone gate that led to a bowl-shaped hole <u>gouged</u> into the ground.

In the middle of the docking bay sat an old, <u>battered</u> spaceship. It appeared to have been <u>fashioned</u> from the spare parts of ancient space wrecks. Solo stood at the side of his ship. He had a big smile on his face.

Luke stopped and looked at the Millennium Falcon. He could not believe his eyes. "What a piece of junk!" he shouted.

Han looked sharply at Luke. How long would these insults last? "It will make point five past light speed," Solo said proudly. "It may not look like much but it moves!

"I've made a lot of special changes in the engines myself. But we're a little rushed, so if you'll get on board, we'll get out of here."

Solo waved for Kenobi, Luke, Threepio, and Artoo to board the ship. Inside, Chewbacca had dropped into the co-pilot's chair. His huge body made it look like a toy. Despite his <u>enormous</u> size, Chewbacca's hands moved quickly over the control panel in front of him. His giant fingers turned <u>minute</u> knobs and wheels.

the Millenium Falcon

The others aboard the ship had strapped themselves into the passenger seats. Kenobi took the time to look around the cabin of the ship. It was not much different from the outside.

"The Millennium Falcon is not a very fancy ship," Kenobi thought. "This could prove to be an interesting trip."

The foursome settled down to wait for Han Solo to complete his outside check of the ship. Soon they would be on their way.

SEQUENCE

You will not believe what happened to us. Even BEFORE we got into the air, we had trouble. Stormtroopers fired at us right AFTER we boarded the ship. Quiet, Artoo, allow me to speak FIRST.

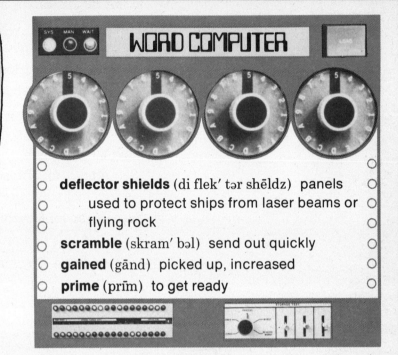

WORD COMPUTER

○ **deflector shields** (di flek′ tər shēldz) panels used to protect ships from laser beams or flying rock
○ **scramble** (skram′ bəl) send out quickly
○ **gained** (gānd) picked up, increased
○ **prime** (prīm) to get ready

TAKEOFF

SEQUENCE means "order." Some of the special SEQUENCE words are **before**, **after**, **first**, and **last**. SEQUENCE words are TIME words. They tell you **when** things happen. Think about TIME or the ORDER of events as you read the story.

MISSION

For questions 1 to 4, circle the letter of the choice that best answers each question. For questions 5 and 6, write your own answers.

1. What happened after the stormtroopers surrounded the ship?
   a. They passed it.
   b. They charged it.
   c. They painted it.
   d. They fired at it.

2. What was the first order the stranger gave?
   a. "I want the ship captured."
   b. "Those are the ones we're looking for."
   c. "Stop the ship that just left Mos Eisley."
   d. "Scramble your fighters."

3. What happened before the hatch shut?
   a. Solo pushed a button.
   b. He called the Galactic Squadron.
   c. Small pieces of the ship broke off.
   d. The ship pulled away from Mos Eisley.

4. What is the last thing Solo said to Chewbacca?
   a. "Prime the laser weapons."
   b. "Chewie, get us out of here."
   c. "Turn on the deflector shields."
   d. "Let's get as far away from here as we can."

5. What happened after the ship gained power?

   _____

   _____

6. What happened before Han ran up the ramp?

   _____

   _____

The stranger who had first spotted Kenobi and Luke now stood outside Docking Bay 94. "Yes," he thought, "those are surely the ones we're looking for."

Dozens of stormtroopers stood near him. "Come here!" the stranger said to the lead trooper. "I want the ship and everyone in it captured. That means the droids too! This is an important matter. I want no mistakes."

The stormtroopers surrounded the docking bay. Within seconds, they were blasting away at Han Solo. At the sound of the first laser shot, Han drew his own blaster and fired back. Then he ran up the ramp and into the Millennium Falcon.

Within the ship, the sounds of gunfire were also heard. Solo came running into the cabin. He pushed a button and the hatch of the Millennium Falcon slammed shut.

"Chewie, get us out of here!" Han shouted above the crash of weapons. He was out of breath, and his own weapon still smoked in his hand.

Slowly, the ship gained power and began to rise. Small pieces, then larger chunks of the ship broke off as stormtroopers' shots found their mark. The ship pulled up and away from Mos Eisley.

The stranger spoke once again into his radio. He called the nearest Galactic Fighter Squadron. "Commander, I want the ship that just left Mos Eisley stopped. Scramble your fighters! That ship must be destroyed!"

Aboard the Millennium Falcon Solo was snapping out orders. "Chewie, turn on the deflector shields. Prime the laser weapons. Let's get as far away from here as we can."

Chewie turns on the deflector shields.

Just a moment, Artoo. BEFORE we read on, there's something we must do FIRST. Oh, Artoo, you *do* know what it is. That's right, we read the questions BEFORE we read the story, not AFTER.

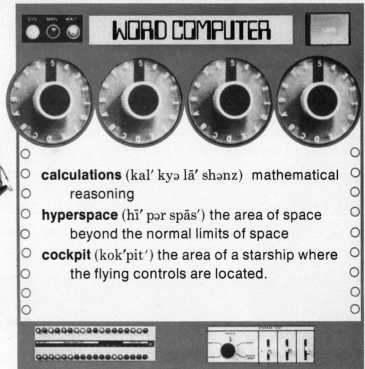

WORD COMPUTER

calculations (kal′ kyə lā′ shənz) mathematical reasoning

hyperspace (hī′ pər spās′) the area of space beyond the normal limits of space

cockpit (kok′pit′) the area of a starship where the flying controls are located.

FLIGHT PLAN Think about the SEQUENCE of events as you read. Knowing **when** things happen helps you understand the story.

MISSION For questions 1 to 4, circle the letter of the choice that best completes each sentence. For questions 5 and 6, write your own answers.

1. The first thing that happened was that _____.
   a. Luke entered the cockpit
   b. Ben strapped himself in
   c. Han sat in the pilot's chair
   d. Artoo was strapped in

2. Solo made calculations _____.
   a. after Luke was strapped in
   b. after winning the battle
   c. before he sat down
   d. before making the jump to hyperspace

3. The Millennium Falcon was safe _____.
   a. after entering hyperspace
   b. before it took off
   c. after Luke sat down
   d. before Han made his calculations

4. The last thing that happened was that _____.
   a. Imperial cruisers were spotted
   b. the ship jumped into hyperspace
   c. Threepio was strapped in
   d. Solo pressed several buttons

5. Kenobi and Luke strapped themselves in after _____.

   _____

   _____

6. Just before the ship lost its deflector shield _____.

   _____

   _____

Han climbed into the pilot's chair. He pressed several buttons on a small computer set into the chair's arm.

A huge shape flashed across the nose of the Millennium Falcon. Then another, and another. "Imperial cruisers," Han said to Chewie. "Our passengers must be hotter than I thought. Chewie, try to hold those cruisers off. I've got to make the calculations for the jump to light speed."

Luke and Kenobi squeezed their way into the small cockpit. "What's up?" Luke asked. "Those ships looked like Imperial cruisers."

"They sure are, my friend." Solo answered. "And they'd like nothing better than to blast us to space dust."

Luke spoke to Solo in a teasing tone. "Why don't you just outrun them? I thought you said this thing was fast."

Solo snapped, "We'll be safe enough once we make the jump to hyperspace."

"How long will that take?" Luke asked.

"A few minutes," Solo said.

A red light began flashing on the control panel. "What's that?" Luke shouted.

"We're losing a deflector shield," Solo said calmly. Laser blasts from the Imperial cruisers were getting closer and closer.

"Strap yourselves in," Solo ordered Kenobi and Luke. "I'm going to make the jump to light speed."

Threepio and Artoo were already strapped into their chairs. As Kenobi and Luke strapped themselves in, Threepio's voice was heard loud and clear. "Oh my," he said, "I'd forgotten how much I hated space travel."

Before the words were fully out of the golden droid's mouth, the ship stopped for a split-second in outer space. Then a powerful force pulled, then pushed the Millennium Falcon. It jumped into hyperspace at light speed.

Han spots Imperial cruisers.

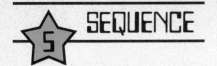

SOLO

Do this part of the lesson on your own. Follow the steps that you used in the other parts of this lesson. May the Force be with you!

WORD COMPUTER

shocked (shokd) surprised
upset (up'set) anger
threat (thret) warning of trouble
weird (wērd) strange; odd
strategy (strat'i jē) method

MISSION

For questions 1 to 4, circle the letter of the choice that best answers each question. For questions 5 and 6, write your own answers.

1. When did Artoo let Chewbacca win the game?
   a. after Luke's lesson
   b. before entering hyperspace
   c. after Han's warning
   d. before the cruisers left

2. Which happened last?
   a. Han spoke to Threepio.
   b. Luke asked about the Force.
   c. Chewie won the game.
   d. Kenobi felt ill.

3. At whom did Chewbacca smile first?
   a. Han
   b. Luke
   c. Artoo
   d. Kenobi

4. What would Luke have to do before he could use the lightsaber well?
   a. be in a battle
   b. learn to relax
   c. win a game
   d. use the Force

5. What happened at the end of the story?

   _____

   _____

6. What might a Wookiee do after losing a game?

   _____

   _____

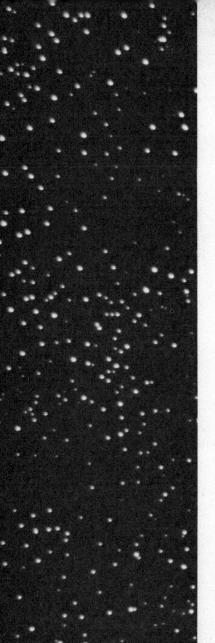

The Millennium Falcon shot through hyperspace. All seemed safe. The threat of the Imperial cruisers was far gone. Chewie and Artoo sat at an odd game table. They were playing a game of chess. However, in this case the chess pieces seemed to be alive. The little droid was winning the game easily.

Solo wandered into the cabin. "You'd better let the Wookiee win," he said. "Don't upset him."

Threepio looked shocked. "But sir," Threepio said, "nobody worries about upsetting a droid."

Solo answered with a knowing smile. "That's because a droid won't pull people's arms out of their sockets when they lose. Wookiees are known to do that."

A now-worried Threepio whispered a message to Artoo. "I suggest a new strategy, Artoo. Let the Wookiee win."

Chewie seemed to like the idea. He smiled first at Han, then at the others as he easily won the rest of the game.

At the far end of the cabin Luke stood with his father's lightsaber held high above him. Luke was trying to learn the fighting skills of a Jedi. Kenobi stood at his side. "Relax, Luke," the old Jedi said. "Remember a Jedi can feel the Force flowing through his body."

"Does it control you?" Luke asked.

"Yes," Kenobi said, "but it also obeys your commands."

Han watched the lesson for a moment. Then he spoke. "Weird beliefs and out-of-date weapons are no match for a good blaster," he said.

"I've flown from one side of the galaxy to the other. I've never seen anything to make me believe in the Force. It's all a lot of nonsense."

Just then Kenobi stopped. He looked ill. The old man held his hand over his heart.

"Are you all right? What's wrong?" asked Luke. Kenobi fell back, then sat still.

The Wookiee wins at chess.

CAUSE AND EFFECT

I wonder what could have been the CAUSE of Ben Kenobi's illness. Have you any ideas, Artoo? Whatever the CAUSE was, the EFFECT on Kenobi was awful. What could it have been?

WORD COMPUTER

whirling (hwûrl'ing) spinning
sub-light engines (sub līt' en'jənz) used for travel at less than light speed
fantastic (fan tas' tik) unbelievable

TAKEOFF

Actions or events do not happen by themselves. Something makes them happen, or CAUSES them. The ACTION or EVENT is called an EFFECT. Read the story carefully to find out what CAUSES things to happen.

MISSION

For questions 1 to 4, circle the letter of the choice that best completes each sentence. For questions 5 and 6, write your own answers.

1. The cause of the ship's bouncing and swaying was ___.
   a. a light began to flash
   b. a button was pushed
   c. a meteor shower
   d. Solo was puzzled

2. One cause of the ship's slowing down was ___.
   a. Kenobi called upon the Force.
   b. Chewie pressed a button.
   c. Alderaan was gone.
   d. Threepio was silent.

3. An effect of traveling at high speeds was ___.
   a. Chewie cut in the sub-light engines
   b. Kenobi became ill

   c. Alderaan disappeared
   d. objects in space seemed to move quickly

4. The effect of Luke's practice was that he ___.
   a. became a teacher
   b. was soon tired
   c. became more skillful
   d. hurt himself badly

5. Not slowing the ship down properly could cause it to ___.

   _____

6. One effect of Alderaan's destruction was that Solo was ___.

   _____

In a few moments, Kenobi seemed to recover. The lesson continued. With practice and Kenobi's teaching, Luke began to use the lightsaber more skillfully.

A small light on the far side of the cabin began to flash. "You'd better strap in. It looks like we're coming up on Alderaan," Solo announced.

Solo and Chewie left the cabin. They walked quickly forward toward the cockpit. From inside the Millennium Falcon objects in space seemed to move at a fantastic speed. The Millennium Falcon had passed through thousands of light years in only a few hours.

"Now comes the tricky part," Solo said to Chewie. "Let's slow down without breaking the ship apart.

"Stand by, Chewie, here we go. Cut in the sub-light engines."

The Wookiee pushed a button on the control panel. At the same time, Solo pulled back on a large control stick set into the cockpit floor.

The long streaks of light that had been shooting past the cockpit began to slow down. The Millennium Falcon seemed to slow to a crawl. The space in front of the ship was filled with rocks and chunks of metal. They rained down upon the spaceship like giant raindrops. The Millennium Falcon bounced and swayed in space.

Luke and Kenobi in the cockpit

Luke and Kenobi rushed to the cockpit. "What's going on?" Luke shouted.

Solo answered quietly. There was a puzzled look on his face. "I don't know. We've come out of hyperspace and into a meteor shower. It's not on any of our maps. It shouldn't even be here, but it is."

"But where is Alderaan?" Luke asked.

"It should be here," Solo added, "We're where we **should** be, but Alderaan isn't."

"What do you mean it isn't there?" Luke asked. "Where is it?"

"That's what I'm trying to tell you," Han said coldly. "It isn't there. It's gone! It's been destroyed!"

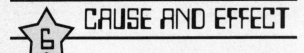

⬢ 6 CAUSE AND EFFECT

> Artoo, between the two of us, what do you think was the CAUSE of Alderaan's destruction? No, I don't know either. But whatever the CAUSE was, it surely had quite an EFFECT on Alderaan.

WORD COMPUTER

careless (kâr′ lis) not careful
confirmed (kən fûrmd′) proven

FLIGHT PLAN

A CAUSE leads to an EFFECT. The CAUSE of an action or event must always happen before the EFFECT. For example, Alderaan has been destroyed. The Empire CAUSED its destruction. It is important to understand the CAUSE of an event.

MISSION

For questions 1 to 4, circle the letter of the choice that best answers each question. For questions 5 and 6, write your own answers.

1. What caused Solo to say, "This could be trouble"?
   a. radio signals
   b. Chewie's warning
   c. alarm bells
   d. laser shots

2. What was one effect of the TIE fighter streaking away?
   a. It seemed to grow smaller.
   b. It fired at the Millennium Falcon.
   c. Luke was hurt.
   d. Han fired lasers at it.

3. What caused the laser explosion outside the cockpit?
   a. the starfleet
   b. a thousand ships
   c. the Millennium Falcon
   d. a TIE fighter

4. What was the effect of Alderaan's destruction upon Luke?
   a. He felt angry.
   b. He felt sick.
   c. He felt happy.
   d. He felt nothing.

5. What was the cause of Alderaan's being destroyed?

   _____

6. What was the effect of Han's increasing his ship's speed?

   _____

Luke felt sick. The thought of an entire planet being gone was more than he could believe. "But how? How could that be?" he asked.

"Alderaan was destroyed by the Empire," Kenobi said. He looked calm, but his voice was hard.

The shower of rocks seemed to be thinning out, but this was no time to be careless. Solo spoke to Kenobi without turning from the controls. "The entire starfleet couldn't destroy the whole planet. It would take a thousand ships with more firepower than . . ."

The scream of alarm bells interrupted Solo's words.

"There's another ship coming in." Solo said. "This could be trouble."

"It's an Imperial fighter," Kenobi said. The truth of his words was confirmed. A bright laser explosion burst outside the cockpit window.

A tiny Imperial TIE fighter streaked past the Millennium Falcon. In an instant it was almost out of sight.

"It must have followed us," Luke offered.

"No, it's a short-range fighter," Kenobi said.

"Short-range?" Solo said. "Where would it come from? There are no bases around here."

Luke watched the tiny dot growing smaller in space. "It sure is leaving in a big hurry. If they can tell someone where we are we haven't got a chance."

Solo was getting angry. "Not if I can help it. Chewie, jam that fighter's radio signals. We'll catch it and knock it out of space."

"You may as well let it go," Kenobi said. "It's too far away. It's almost out of range."

"Not for long!" Solo shouted. He increased the Millennium Falcon's speed. The ship rocketed forward. Soon it was on the trail of the little TIE fighter.

the TIE fighter

⬡6 CAUSE AND EFFECT

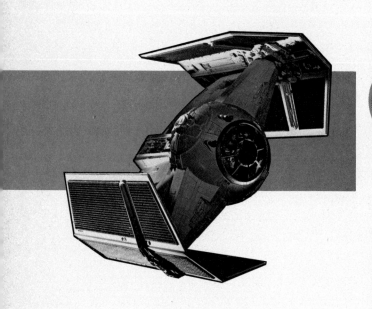

SOLO ●
Do this part of the lesson on your own. Follow the steps that you used in the other parts of this lesson. May the Force be with you!

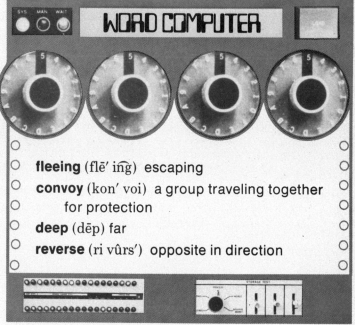

WORD COMPUTER

fleeing (flē′ iṅg) escaping
convoy (kon′ voi) a group traveling together for protection
deep (dēp) far
reverse (ri vûrs′) opposite in direction

MISSION
For questions 1 to 4, circle the letter of the choice that best completes each sentence. For questions 5 and 6, write your own answers.

1. The cause of the ship's being pulled in was _____.
   a. the Force
   b. Han's controls
   c. a tractor beam
   d. Darth Vader

2. Han asked Chewie to _____.
   a. turn the ship around
   b. blast the moon
   c. land on the moon
   d. have Luke sit down

3. The cause of Kenobi's worry was that he knew _____.
   a. the TIE fighter was small
   b. Han was ready for battle
   c. Chewie was a poor pilot
   d. the "moon" was a space station

4. An effect of coming closer to the moon was that the moon _____.
   a. moved more quickly
   b. looked larger
   c. stood still
   d. fired lasers

5. Two possible causes Luke gave for the TIE fighter being deep in space were _____.

   _____

   _____

6. The effect of the tractor beam was that _____.

   _____

   _____

40

With its engine wide open, the Millennium Falcon gained on the fleeing fighter. The pilot of the TIE fighter must have known he was being chased. Suddenly, he went into a steep turn and dove. Surprisingly, the Millennium Falcon stayed with the swifter TIE ship.

Solo called upon his co-pilot for help. "More speed, Chewie! We've almost got it in range."

Kenobi leaned forward. His eyes searched the skies ahead. "A fighter that small couldn't get this deep into space on its own."

"Then he must have gotten lost, or been part of a convoy," Luke said.

Ahead one of the small stars seemed to be getting larger and brighter than the others. Luke began to wonder about it. "Why would one star get so much brighter than the others?" Luke thought.

As the Millennium Falcon got closer to the fighter, the star, which now looked like a small moon, grew even larger.

"Look at him," said Luke. "He's heading for that small moon."

"He'll never make it," Solo snapped. "He's almost in range."

For the first time Kenobi looked worried. "That's not a moon! It's a space station! Turn the ship around!" he shouted.

Han laughed. "It's too big to be a space station," he said. "But maybe you're right, Kenobi. Chewie, full reverse! Turn the ship around. Lock in the extra power drive."

The ship was unable to turn. Even with the extra power drive, it continued to move forward, toward the ever larger "moon."

"We're caught in a tractor beam," Han shouted. "It's pulling us in. There's nothing we can do. I'm shutting the engines down. But they're not getting me without a fight."

The helpless ship and its passengers were pulled up into the huge space station. The Millennium Falcon came to rest deep in the body of the Death Star.

the Millennium Falcon in the docking bay

Oh, Artoo, things are getting worse. Look! Look! It's Vader and Tarkin. They are two people whose evil CHARACTERS we all know. I'm sure they're up to no good.

WORD COMPUTER

remains (ri mānz′) things that are left
abandoned (ə ban′ dend) left
log (log) record of a ship's journey

TAKEOFF

There are many ways an author tells about a CHARACTER. He or she may describe the way a CHARACTER acts in the face of danger — or how the CHARACTER looks when he is afraid. As you read, look for all the ways a CHARACTER is described.

MISSION

For questions 1 to 4, circle the letter of the choice that best answers each question. For questions 5 and 6, write your own answers.

1. What can you tell about Vader?
   a. He likes the Princess.
   b. He likes Tarkin.
   c. He uses people.
   d. He has no family.

2. How does the officer feel about the empty ship?
   a. He believes it is empty.
   b. He is not trusting.
   c. He has tricked Vader.
   d. He has tricked Tarkin.

3. Which does **not** describe Vader?
   a. towering
   b. masked face
   c. white-suited
   d. in command

4. How does Vader feel about what is happening?
   a. He is uneasy.
   b. He is pleased.
   c. He does not care.
   d. He is frightened.

5. Why do you think Vader never finished his thought?

   _____

   _____

6. How can you tell the officer respects Vader?

   _____

   _____

Grand Moff Tarkin and Lord Darth Vader watched the Millennium Falcon on a large viewscreen set into one wall of the Grand Moff's office. It sat silent and still on the floor of Docking Bay 2037. Thirty armed stormtroopers surrounded the ship. Tarkin pushed a button on his desk.

A voice came from beneath the viewscreen. "We've captured a starship entering the remains of the Alderaan system. Its markings match those of a ship that blasted its way out of Mos Eisley."

Vader nodded his head. "Yes, that makes sense," he said. His voice rumbled through the black, metal breath screen. "They must be trying to return the plans to the Princess," the Dark Lord said to Tarkin. "She may yet be of some use to us."

Vader left Tarkin. He made his way down to Docking Bay 2037. As Vader approached the Millennium Falcon, the officer in charge snapped to attention. Then he began to deliver his report.

"There's no one on board, sir. According to the log, the crew abandoned ship right after take-off. It must be a trick, sir. Several of the escape pods have been jettisoned."

Vader and Tarkin

"Did you find any droids aboard?" Vader asked.

"No sir," the officer answered. "If there were any on board, they must also have been jettisoned."

Vader looked up at the Millennium Falcon. Even through his masked face he appeared worried. "Send a search crew aboard," the Dark Lord ordered. "I want every part of this ship checked.

"I feel something is wrong. I don't know what it is. It's something I haven't felt since . . ." The Lord's words trailed off. It was almost as if he did not dare to finish the thought.

"See to it that my orders are carried out," Vader said to the officer. Then the towering figure in black turned and left the docking bay.

CHARACTER

Artoo, I must say that I find your CHARACTER more agreeable now than when we first met. You are much nicer to be with. It has taken you a while to learn that I am always right.

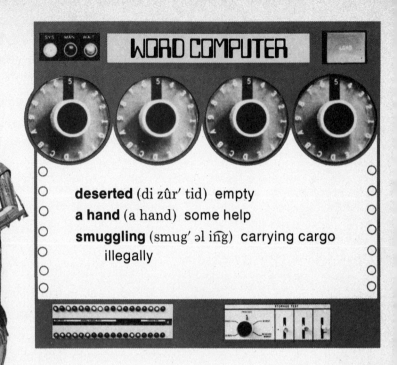

WORD COMPUTER

deserted (di zûr′ tid) empty
a hand (a hand) some help
smuggling (smug′ əl iñg) carrying cargo
   illegally

FLIGHT PLAN

The little pieces that make up a person's CHARACTER are called TRAITS (trāts). TRAITS may be how a person looks (tall, old, young), feels (happy, angry, frightened), or acts (pleasant, evil, greedy). As you read, think about the CHARACTER TRAITS of Han, Luke, Kenobi, and Chewie.

MISSION

For questions 1 to 4, circle the letter of the choice that best completes each sentence. For questions 5 and 6, write your own answers.

1. You can tell that all Han does _____.
   a. is honest
   b. makes him happy
   c. is not honest
   d. pays well

2. The two crewmen who came aboard were not _____.
   a. stormtroopers
   b. well dressed
   c. very tall
   d. alert

3. Kenobi is sure that he can _____.
   a. get Han to like him
   b. knock out the tractor beam
   c. find the Princess
   d. locate the plans

4. It appears that troopers are _____.
   a. very strong
   b. great fighters
   c. not very strong
   d. used to obeying orders

5. You can tell that Chewbacca is strong because he _____.

   _____

   _____

6. Two reasons Luke and Han might have put on the stormtroopers' uniforms are _____.

   _____

   _____

Aboard the Millennium Falcon all was quiet and deserted. Suddenly, two pieces of the ship's floor were lifted. The heads of Han Solo, Luke Skywalker, and Kenobi popped out. Each man looked carefully about him. All was quiet.

Luke was the first to speak. "Boy, it's lucky you had these hidden rooms."

Han smiled. "I use them for smuggling," he said. "I never thought I'd be smuggling myself in them. This whole thing is crazy. Even if I could take off, I'd never get past that tractor beam."

"Leave that to me!" Kenobi said.

"You're a fool, Kenobi. You and that Force of yours can't break a tractor beam," Han said.

"Who is more foolish," Kenobi asked, "the fool or the fool who follows him?"

Han had no answer. He could only shake his head in wonder at the old man. Luke, Kenobi, and Han pulled themselves up. Chewbacca followed. Then he easily lifted the two droids up and onto the ship's floor.

As the trapped space travelers gathered to plan their escape, two of the Death Star's crewmen came aboard. They were there to check the ship out for passengers or droids. Their search did not last long. Han and Chewie quickly knocked them out. That left two stormtroopers to guard the Millennium Falcon.

"Hey down there," Han called out to the troopers. "Come on up and give us a hand."

The troopers, thinking they were helping the crewmen, did as they were ordered. As they stepped through the Millennium Falcon's door, they too were knocked out.

Luke and Han quickly put on the uniforms of the fallen stormtroopers. With Kenobi, Chewbacca, Threepio, and Artoo behind them, the two "stormtroopers" headed deeper into the Death Star.

Stormtroopers on guard

Luke, Han, and Kenobi

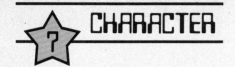

CHARACTER

SOLD ● Do this part of the lesson on your own. Follow the steps that you used in the other parts of the lesson. May the Force be with you!

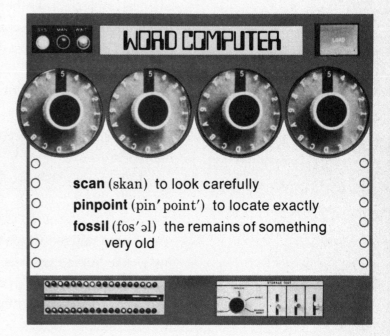

WORD COMPUTER

scan (skan) to look carefully
pinpoint (pin′point′) to locate exactly
fossil (fos′əl) the remains of something very old

MISSION For questions 1 to 4, circle the letter of the choice that best answers each question. For questions 5 and 6, write your own answers.

1. Which best tells about Luke's feeling for Kenobi?
   a. hatred
   b. respect
   c. fear
   d. anger

2. How would you describe Artoo as he was working?
   a. overworked
   b. cheerful
   c. tired
   d. angry

3. What is most important to Kenobi?
   a. the safety of the droids
   b. his own life
   c. the Millennium Falcon
   d. Han's safety

4. Which word best tells about Han's feelings for Kenobi?
   a. hatred
   b. fear
   c. respect
   d. anger

5. What 3 words would describe Ben Kenobi?

   _____

   _____

   _____

6. How do you think Luke felt when Kenobi left?

   _____

   _____

46

They had not gone far when Kenobi took the lead. He led them into a small room. It was filled from floor to ceiling with dials and computers.

Kenobi took a moment to scan the room. He pointed to a small viewscreen. "That's the one," he said. "Threepio, have Artoo plug in over there. He should be able to give us a picture of the entire Imperial computer system."

Artoo rolled over to the viewscreen and plugged himself in. The screen suddenly came to life. It flashed pictures of the most secret parts of the Death Star. Artoo whirred and hummed. Then he chirped a message to Threepio.

"Artoo says he's found the main control for the tractor beam that's holding our ship. He says he'll pinpoint it for you."

The screen lit up again. A bright red light lit one part of the screen. Kenobi studied the lighted diagram. "The tractor beam can be stopped. I don't think any of you can help me. I must go alone."

Luke moved toward Kenobi. "I must go with you," he said.

The old Jedi smiled kindly at Luke. "Be patient. Stay and watch over the droids. They must be delivered safely into Rebel hands."

"Your future lies along a different path from mine. The Force will be with you always!" With that, Kenobi left.

Han shook his head. "Wow! Where did you dig up that old fossil?" he asked.

"Ben . . . Obi-wan Kenobi is a great man," Luke answered with feeling.

"Yeah," Han said in a nasty tone, "great at getting us into trouble."

"Well, what do you think we should do?" Luke asked Han.

"I don't know, kid. I just don't know," Han said as he sat down in the nearest chair.

Kenobi prepares to leave.

INFERENCE

Yes! Yes! Artoo, you are quite right. You are very important in this part of the story. You don't have to tell us why, Artoo!

WORD COMPUTER

executed (ek′ sə kyo͞ot əd)   killed
imagine (i maj′ in) to suppose
glory (glôr′ ē) fame or honor
gleam (glēm) shine

TAKEOFF

An INFERENCE is very much like a good guess. You can use the facts of a story to help you make an INFERENCE. An INFERENCE is not a **wild** guess. It is a guess that you make using facts in the story.

MISSION

For questions 1 to 4, circle the letter of the choice that best completes each sentence. For questions 5 and 6, write your own answers.

1. You can infer that when Artoo whistles and beeps he is _____.
   a. overheated
   b. unhappy
   c. excited
   d. dreaming

2. You can tell that Han is not really _____.
   a. a good fighter
   b. anxious to fight
   c. who he says he is
   d. a pilot

3. It would appear that Han is _____.
   a. careless
   b. sad
   c. sleepy
   d. greedy

4. From Luke's actions, you know he feels that rescuing Leia is _____.
   a. important
   b. frightening
   c. easy
   d. unimportant

5. Luke asks Han for help because _____.

_____

_____

6. After Solo rescues the Princess, he hopes she will _____.

_____

_____

Artoo whistled and beeped for several seconds. He was very excited. "What is it?" asked Luke.

Threepio answered Luke's question. "I'm afraid I'm not quite sure, sir. He says 'I found her' and keeps repeating 'She's here.'"

"Who has he found?" Luke asked.

"Artoo says he's found Princess Leia," Threepio continued. "She's on Level Five, Cell 2187. And I'm afraid she's soon to be executed!"

"Oh, no," shouted Luke. "We've got to do something."

Solo began to take an interest in what was happening. "Now, look," he said, "let's not get any funny ideas. Kenobi said to wait right here."

Luke was so excited he could hardly speak. "But Kenobi didn't know she was here. Look, all we have to do is get into that cell block and rescue her."

Solo looked at Luke. "I'm not going anywhere," he said. "I was paid to take you people to Alderaan. Now, there's no Alderaan, so there's no deal! I work for money, kid—not glory!"

"But they're going to kill her," Luke begged. "Help me!"

"I'd rather they kill her than me," Solo said coldly.

Luke begs Solo to help him.

"She's rich," Luke said teasingly. "Rich and powerful! Listen, if you were the one to rescue her, the reward would be more than you can imagine."

Solo looked interested. "I can imagine quite a bit," Solo said with a gleam in his eyes. "All right, kid. Chewie and I will help you out. But you better be right about this! What's your plan?"

Luke looked puzzled for a moment. Then he said, "Okay, here's what we'll do . . . ."

☆8 INFERENCE

Artoo, why are you jumping up and down like that? I have only the FACT that you are beeping and chirping. So I can INFER that you must be excited about something.

WORD COMPUTER

handcuffs (hand′ kufs) metal rings placed around the hands

escort (es′ kôrt) to go along with someone

fate (fāt) something that happens to a person

FLIGHT PLAN

To make an INFERENCE, you use information, or facts, that you already know. These facts could be things characters in the story have said or done. By making an INFERENCE you are deciding what is most likely true.

MISSION

For questions 1 to 4, circle the letter of the choice that best answers each question. For questions 5 and 6, write your own answers.

1. Why were the droids left behind?
   a. They were to go to Alderaan.
   b. They were to radio the Rebels.
   c. They would not be needed.
   d. They were afraid of Vader.

2. How does the officer feel about Wookiees?
   a. He respects them.
   b. He does not like them.
   c. He worships them.
   d. He has never seen one.

3. What can you infer about most storm-troopers?
   a. They are tall.
   b. They are smart.
   c. They are weak.
   d. They are trusting.

4. What best describes Han's shooting skill?
   a. a slow shot
   b. a poor shot
   c. a good shot
   d. a fair shot

5. What was the meaning of Han's warning?

   _____

   _____

6. What might have happened if the officer had used the wall phone?

   _____

   _____

Luke's plan was simple. First, Chewbacca's hands would be placed in steel handcuffs to make him look like a prisoner. Then Luke and Han, wearing their stolen stormtrooper uniforms, would escort Chewie to the cell block where Leia was being held prisoner. With Chewie as a "prisoner," Luke hoped to fool the guards into opening the cell door. Then, Luke, Han, and Chewie would rescue the Princess.

While the Princess was being rescued, Threepio and Artoo would stay behind and wait.

The trio completed the trip to the cell block with surprising ease. An elevator led directly to the cell block. A stormtrooper stood near the open elevator door staring at the giant Wookiee prisoner. "Where are you taking this **thing**?" the officer asked. "I'll have to clear this prisoner."

He reached for a wall phone but his hand never touched it. A blast from Han's laser rifle dropped him quickly. Other guards hearing the shot raced into the small room. In seconds, they too shared the officer's fate.

"Let's find the Princess and get out of here," Han yelled to Luke.

Luke ran down the long cell corridor. He checked each cell door for the number he wanted. He did not find it until he was almost halfway down the corridor. The door was locked tightly, but a long blast from Luke's laser pistol opened it quickly.

Inside the cell Luke saw Princess Leia Organa. She was even more beautiful than her picture. She looked at Luke in his white stormtrooper uniform.

"Aren't you a little short for a stormtrooper?" she asked Luke.

Luke pulled off his helmet. He was stunned by the Princess's beauty. "What?" he asked. "Oh—the uniform. I'm not really a stormtrooper. I'm Luke Skywalker and I'm here to rescue you. I'm here with Kenobi."

From the corridor, Han called out a warning. "Hurry up, Luke. It looks like we've got company!"

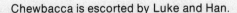

Chewbacca is escorted by Luke and Han.

Leia in her prison cell

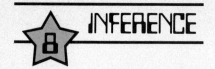

INFERENCE 8

SOLO ● Do this part of the lesson on your own. Follow the steps that you used in the other parts of the lesson. May the Force be with you!

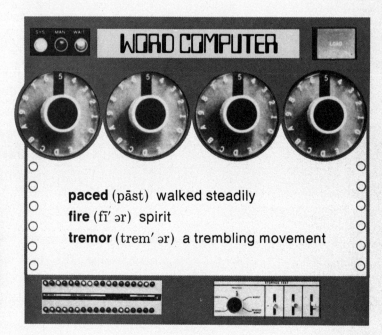

WORD COMPUTER

paced (pāst) walked steadily
fire (fī′ ər) spirit
tremor (trem′ ər) a trembling movement

MISSION For questions 1 to 4, circle the letter of the choice that best completes each sentence. For questions 5 and 6, write your own answers.

1. It appears that the Force _____.
   a. does not affect Tarkin
   b. affects Tarkin
   c. does not affect Vader
   d. affects the Princess

2. You can infer that the Princess _____.
   a. was in cell 2187
   b. escaped from the Death Star
   c. set off the alarm
   d. called Tarkin

3. From Tarkin's words, you can tell that he _____.
   a. fears the Rebels
   b. fears Vader
   c. does not fear Kenobi
   d. fears the droids

4. Vader most likely wants to meet Kenobi to _____.
   a. ignore him
   b. speak with him
   c. eat with him
   d. fight with him

5. Tarkin feels that the Jedis are _____.

   _____

   _____

6. Vader's feelings about Kenobi are _____.

   _____

   _____

The Grand Moff Tarkin watched Darth Vader. The Dark Lord of the Sith was pacing around the large room.

Finally, Vader stopped. He looked about as though a great bell had sounded. Then he turned to Tarkin. "He is here! Obi-wan Kenobi is aboard the Death Star."

"Obi-wan Kenobi!" Tarkin said. "Why, that's impossible. What makes you think so?"

Vader looked closely at Tarkin. "I felt a tremor in the Force. The last time I felt it was when I was with my old master, Obi-wan Kenobi."

Tarkin smiled evilly. "Surely he must be dead by now. The Jedis have all been hunted down by the soldiers of the Empire. You yourself had a great hand in it. And even if he did escape, he would be dead now of old age, or too weak to harm us."

"Perhaps," Vader answered, "but one can never be sure. Kenobi was strong in the ways of the Force. Do not think lightly of the Force . . . or of the powers of a Jedi!"

Tarkin shook his head sadly at Vader's words. "The Jedis are gone. Their fire has gone out of the galaxy. You are the only Jedi left."

A speaker on Tarkin's desk began to hum. A voice announced very troubling news. "Governor Tarkin, we have an emergency alert on Level Five, cell 2187. Repeat. We have an emergency . . . ."

"The Princess!" Tarkin shouted. "Vader, sound all alarms!"

Vader made no move to follow the Governor's order. "I was right," the figure in black said. "Obi-wan **is** here. The Force is with him."

"If you're right, he must not be allowed to escape," Tarkin said. "Sound the alarm, Vader!"

"Escape is not his plan," the Dark Lord hissed. "I must face my old master alone!" Then he sounded the alarm.

Vader prepares to sound the alarm.

Oh, Artoo, I'm glad Master Luke left us behind. Given my love for peace and quiet I can only CONCLUDE that I would have been most unhappy in the cell block.

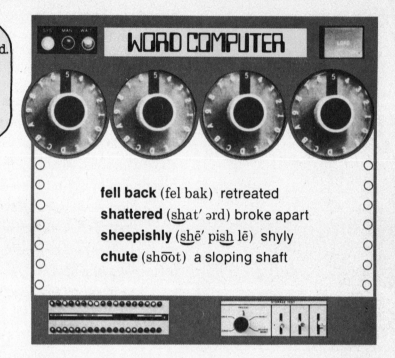

WORD COMPUTER

fell back (fel bak) retreated
shattered (shat′ ərd) broke apart
sheepishly (shē′ pish lē) shyly
chute (shoot) a sloping shaft

TAKEOFF

When you use a step-by-step method to decide what has happened, is happening, or will happen, you are DRAWING A CONCLUSION. You can reach a CONCLUSION only after studying the facts. A CONCLUSION is more than a guess. It is based on what you have read.

MISSION

For questions 1 to 4, circle the letter of the choice that best answers each question. For questions 5 and 6, write your own answers.

1. What can you conclude about laser rays?
   a. They can kill.
   b. They are all red.
   c. They travel slowly.
   d. They kill only stormtroopers.

2. What is it like in the garbage pit?
   a. hard
   b. wet
   c. oily
   d. rocky

3. What conclusion can you draw about Luke?
   a. Luke did not plan the escape.
   b. He has planned many escapes.
   c. Luke doesn't like planning escapes.
   d. He has not planned any other escapes.

4. What conclusion can you draw about the Princess?
   a. She frightens easily.
   b. She is afraid of battle.
   c. She has courage.
   d. She dislikes Luke.

5. How did Luke think the escape would be?

   _____

   _____

6. Why did the Princess shoot a hole in the wall?

   _____

   _____

Luke and Princess Leia ran from the cell and down the corridor, where they joined Han and Chewie. "Who are they?" the Princess demanded. Before Luke could answer, a large explosion ripped open the elevator door. A squad of stormtroopers blasted their way into the cell block.

Solo and Chewie shot back at them. Soon the small room was filled with countless deadly laser rays. Smoke and flame were everywhere. Slowly Han, Chewie, Luke, and Leia fell back down the corridor.

Luke called Threepio on a small radio. "We've been cut off!" Luke screamed into the radio. "Are there any other ways out of the cell block?"

Threepio's voice came back carrying bad news. "The elevator is the only way out. The whole ship has heard the alarm. I am sorry, sir, but it looks to me as if you're trapped."

Artoo and Threepio try to help.

"Trapped!" Han yelled. "I can't hold them off forever!" To prove the truth of Han's words, red energy bolts shattered the wall behind him.

The Princess could not believe what was happening. "This is some rescue," she said angrily. "When you came in here didn't you have a plan for getting out?"

"Don't ask me," Han answered. "Luke here is the smart one."

Luke smiled a silly grin. "Well, I'm new at planning escapes," he said sheepishly. "I thought getting out would be easy."

Before Luke could fire another shot, the Princess grabbed his laser pistol. She shot a large hole in the wall next to them.

"Somebody has to save our skins," Leia shouted over the explosions of laser bolts. "Into the garbage chute, boys!"

With that, the Princess jumped feet first into the chute. She was followed quickly by Luke, an unhappy Chewie, and Han.

Four splashes signalled their arrival at the bottom of the garbage chute.

⭐ 9 DRAWING CONCLUSIONS

Artoo, our friends are surely in a frightful mess. And what a way to end it all! Oh my! I can only CONCLUDE that our friends are in deep trouble.

WORD COMPUTER

compactor (kom pak′ tər) a machine that grinds garbage
rumbling (rum′ bliñg) a deep, heavy sound
serpent sûr′ pənt) a snake

FLIGHT PLAN

When you DRAW A CONCLUSION you first look carefully at the facts. This is the method a detective uses to solve a mystery. A good detective uses the right clues. A good reader uses the right facts.

MISSION

For questions 1 to 4, circle the choice that best completes each sentence. For questions 5 and 6, write your own answers.

1. You can conclude that Luke _____.
   a. had seen other serpents
   b. wanted to find more serpents
   c. was surprised by the serpent
   d. did not see the serpent

2. You can draw the conclusion that the "deep rumbling" came from _____.
   a. Artoo Detoo
   b. Luke
   c. the moving walls
   d. Luke's radio

3. If Artoo shut down the compactors, _____.
   a. the walls would stop moving
   b. Vader would get the plans
   c. stormtroopers would appear
   d. Threepio would be hurt

4. Han had a "bad feeling" about _____.
   a. the Millennium Falcon
   b. finding more snakes
   c. the safety of the Princess
   d. the walls coming together.

5. You can conclude that if Threepio doesn't hear the message _____.

   _____

   _____

6. If the walls do come together, you can conclude that _____.

   _____

   _____

The room Luke and his friends had jumped into was a garbage compactor. They had barely escaped the deadly fire of the stormtroopers. But now the four were not much better off. They stood in a locked room, knee deep in garbage and muck.

Han looked at the Princess and made a deep bow. "Oh! The garbage chute was really a great idea. Let's get out of here."

Han pulled out his blaster and fired a shot at the locked door. The laser blast hit the door and then bounced off the walls several times.

Suddenly Luke jumped out of the muck. "There's something alive in here!" he screamed. "Something just brushed against my leg."

A long ugly head popped out of the garbage. It looked around, then ducked out of sight. Seconds later, Luke was pulled under.

As suddenly as he was pulled under, Luke reappeared. The huge serpent was wrapped all about Luke's body. Solo fired two quick shots at the beast. Both shots hit their mark and it died.

Luke was covered from head to toe with garbage, but he was safe. Before Luke had climbed back on his feet, he heard a deep rumbling sound. Slowly, but steadily, the walls began to move closer together.

"I've got a very bad feeling about this," Han said softly.

Leia once again took charge. "Grab those long poles," she commanded. "Try to brace the walls with them." The men did as they were told, but it did not help. The powerful walls moved closer and closer.

Luke grabbed his radio. "Threepio! Threepio! Come in, Threepio! Have Artoo shut down all the garbage compactors!" Luke repeated his message over and over, but the only answer he received was silence.

Where were Threepio and Artoo?

Luke and his friends in the garbage compactor

⭐9 DRAWING CONCLUSIONS

SOLO

● Do this part of the lesson on your own. Follow the steps that you used in the other parts of this lesson. May the Force be with you!

WORD COMPUTER

overheat (ō'vər hēt') to become too hot
taken the liberty (tā'kən thə lib'ər tē) acted on one's own
crush (krush) to squash

MISSION

For questions 1 to 4, circle the letter of the choice that best answers each question. For questions 5 and 6, write your own answers.

1. What can you conclude about the repair shop?
   a. It is above Leia's cell.
   b. Droids are fixed there.
   c. It has a great many tools.
   d. It is below the control room

2. Why did Threepio direct Artoo into the second control room?
   a. It had the needed controls.
   b. It was closer to the repair shop.
   c. It contained the plans to the Death Star.
   d. The walls stopped moving.

3. What conclusion can you draw about Threepio's hearing?
   a. It is not as good as a human's.
   b. It is better than a machine's.
   c. It is better than a human's.
   d. It is not as good as a machine's.

4. What might have happened if Threepio had not fooled the trooper?
   a. The trooper would have been blasted.
   b. The walls would have crushed everyone.
   c. Lord Vader would have discovered the Millennium Falcon
   d. Artoo would have escaped with the plans.

5. What might have happened if Artoo had waited a few minutes longer?

   _____

   _____

6. Why must Luke have felt tired, but happy?

   _____

   _____

In the control room, the sound of Luke's voice could hardly be heard by the human ear. However, Threepio was not human, he was a machine. The golden droid easily picked up Luke's frightened cries for help.

He would have liked to help, but at this time Threepio needed help himself. An armed stormtrooper entered the little room in search of the escaped Princess. The soldier looked at the two droids.

Threepio thought fast and well. "Come with me, Artoo," he said. The two droids moved toward the soldier, who was aiming his blaster at them.

"Will you excuse us, sir," Threepio said to the trooper. "All this noise and fighting has caused the wires and tubes in my little friend here to overheat. If you will be kind enough to step aside, sir, I will take him below for repairs."

Threepio did not wait for an answer. "Come along, you," he said to the unusually quiet Artoo. The two droids passed out of the room.

Threepio directed Artoo into another room much like the one they had just left.

Far below, the walls of the compactor room had almost come together. In another moment the moving walls would meet and crush the four people in it.

In the small control room, Threepio begged the smaller droid to hurry. "Be quick about it, Artoo," he ordered. "Plug into the garbage compactor system. Master Luke and our new friends are in great danger!"

Artoo plugged himself into a wall socket as Luke's words came over the radio. "Threepio!" Luke screamed. "Shut down all the garbage compactors on the cell level. We have no time to . . ."

Threepio's words came to Luke over the radio in his hand. "Artoo has done as you wished, sir," the voice said. "The compactors have been shut down. And, sir, I have taken the liberty to have Artoo open the compactor door as well."

Luke felt suddenly tired, but he had never been so happy in his life.

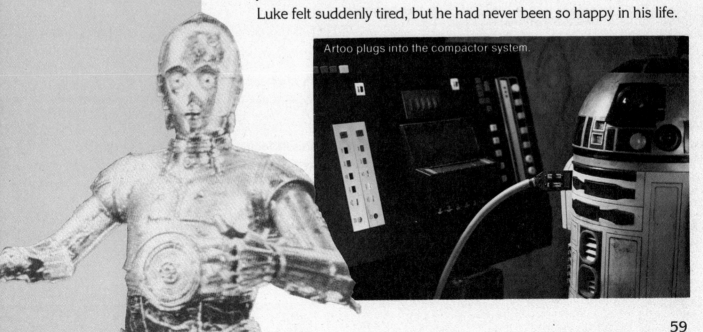

Artoo plugs into the compactor system.

FACT AND OPINION

Oh, Artoo, look at Kenobi. He's so high up in the air. I bet that would make me ill. Is that a FACT? No, Artoo, that is my OPINION. I believe that it would make me ill.

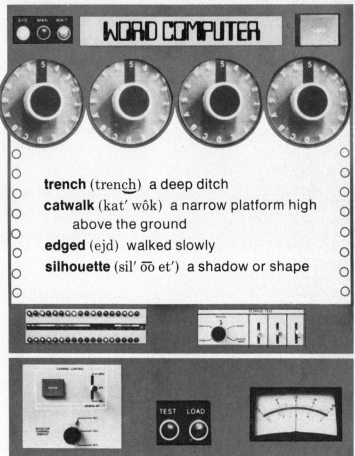

WORD COMPUTER

trench (trench) a deep ditch

catwalk (kat' wôk) a narrow platform high above the ground

edged (ejd) walked slowly

silhouette (sil' oo et') a shadow or shape

TAKEOFF

A FACT is the opposite of an OPINION. A FACT can be proven. It is something that has existed or has happened. An OPINION is a belief **about** something. It could also be the way you feel about something.

MISSION

Read each statement below. If it is a FACT, circle the word FACT. If it is an OPINION, circle the word OPINION.

1. The trooper thought he heard something.
   FACT   OPINION

2. The corridor was dimly lit.
   FACT   OPINION

3. Kenobi would have been seen if he hadn't ducked.
   FACT   OPINION

4. The silhouette meant certain danger.
   FACT   OPINION

5. The dials changed from red to blue.
   FACT   OPINION

6. The silhouette was behind Kenobi.
   FACT   OPINION

Ben Kenobi stood on a narrow catwalk thousands of feet in the air, high above an open power trench. Slowly, he edged his way along the catwalk. His goal, the control lever for the tractor beam, was almost in reach. A few more careful steps and Kenobi's hands touched the control lever. He pushed the lever to the "off" setting. On the control panel before him, the dials changed color from red to blue.

"There," thought Kenobi, "that does it. The tractor beam is shut off. Now, the Millennium Falcon will be able to escape the Death Star."

A sudden noise caused Kenobi to duck behind the huge control panel. A squad of stormtroopers moved to within several feet of Kenobi. The soldiers looked about, searching for something—or someone.

After a few moments they passed from Kenobi's sight. Quickly, soundlessly, he moved from shadow to shadow. He seemed to be one with the darkness. For an instant he was there. Then he was gone!

"What was that?" a trooper asked.

"I don't know," his leader answered. "Something was there. I know it. But maybe it was more like a **feeling** that something was there."

"Well, whatever it was, it's gone now. Let's get going. Maybe we can find the Princess and those madmen that tried to rescue her. At least we know **they're** real."

The sound of the trooper's footsteps faded away in the distance. Kenobi carefully looked around. Then he stepped into the dimly-lit corridor and started walking down it.

But he failed to see the silhouette that followed close behind him. Who could it be?

the catwalk high above the power trench

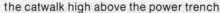

★ 10 FACT AND OPINION

I'll bet Luke and his friends are glad to get out of that garbage. That, Artoo, is my OPINION. No, Artoo, an OPINION does not have to be proven. That's what makes them so easy to form!

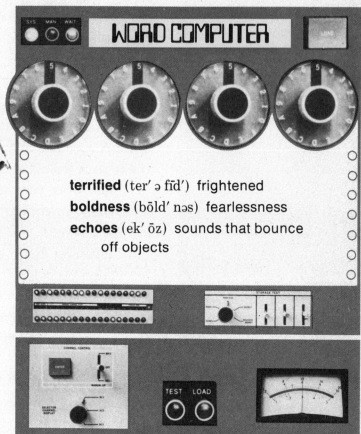

WORD COMPUTER

terrified (ter′ ə fīd′) frightened
boldness (bōld′ nəs) fearlessness
echoes (ek′ ōz) sounds that bounce off objects

FLIGHT PLAN

A FACT is something that is true or real. An OPINION is something that you feel or believe. It may be based on a past experience or an idea. Characters in a story often give their OPINIONS about things that are happening in the story.

MISSION

Read each statement below. If it is a FACT, circle the word FACT. If it is an OPINION, circle the word OPINION.

1. The reward is not worth what Han is going through.
   FACT   OPINION

2. The Millennium Falcon was guarded by stormtroopers.
   FACT   OPINION

3. The Princess feels that Han should listen to her commands.
   FACT   OPINION

4. The door was made of heavy metal.
   FACT   OPINION

5. Han's shooting of the door was not very smart.
   FACT   OPINION

6. Things looked bad for Luke, Han, Chewie, and the Princess.
   FACT   OPINION

The door of the garbage compactor opened. Chewie, the largest and most terrified of the group, was the first one out. He was followed quickly by the Princess, Luke, and Han.

"Where are we?" Luke asked. "I wonder where that door leads?"

"I'll tell you in a minute, kid," Han said. Before anyone could stop him, Han snapped off two quick laser blasts. The heavy metal door was instantly turned to white ash. It fell away as the echoes of the laser blasts bounced along the walls of the corridor behind it.

"Now, they'll know for sure where we are," the Princess said angrily.

She turned and addressed Han. "Listen I don't know who you are, or where you come from, but from now on you do as I tell you!"

Han was stunned by the boldness of the Princess. But he soon recovered. "Look, let's get something straight! I'm Han Solo. I'm captain of the Millennium Falcon, the ship that's going to get us out of here. I don't take orders from anyone."

"It's a miracle you're still alive," the Princess said.

"Somebody get this big monkey out of my way!" the Princess commanded as she pushed past Chewie and started down a long corridor.

Han looked after her and shook his head. "No reward is worth this," he said to Luke. "No reward!"

With that Luke, Han, and Chewie ran to catch up to the rapidly striding Princess. They caught up to her as she rounded a bend in the corridor. The Princess held up her hand in a signal to stop. Then she pointed down through a large window.

Below them was the silent form of the Millennium Falcon. It was guarded by a great many stormtroopers. Things looked really bad. How would they ever get back into the ship?

Luke, Leia, and Han

⭐ 10 FACT AND OPINION

SOLO
● Do this part of the lesson on your own. Follow the steps that you used in the other parts of the lesson. May the Force be with you!

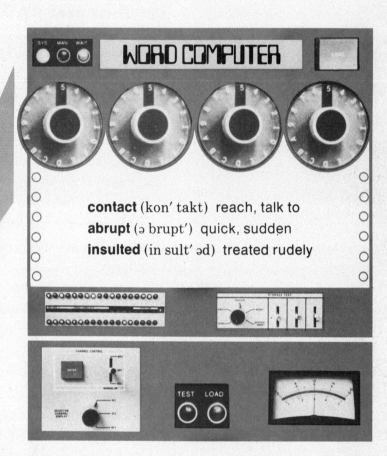

WORD COMPUTER

contact (kon′ takt) reach, talk to
abrupt (ə brupt′) quick, sudden
insulted (in sult′ əd) treated rudely

MISSION
Read each **statement** below. If it is a FACT, circle the word FACT. If it is an OPINION, circle the word OPINION.

1. Solo shouted at the troopers in several languages.
   FACT   OPINION

2. Twenty armed troopers marched down the corridor.
   FACT   OPINION

3. Solo's shouts were fearsome.
   FACT   OPINION

4. Leia believed the Millennium Falcon was a "flying wreck."
   FACT   OPINION

5. Solo's first shots killed two troopers.
   FACT   OPINION

6. Luke thinks Solo is not very smart.
   FACT   OPINION

7. Threepio feels he is safe for the moment.
   FACT   OPINION

8. Solo led the others down the corridor.
   FACT   OPINION

While the others looked down upon the Millennium Falcon and the soldiers that guarded it, Luke was trying to contact the droids. "See Threepio! See Threepio!" he called. "Do you hear me? Come in, See Threepio!"

"Yes, Luke," came the golden droid's reply. "We are safe for the moment, sir. Artoo and I are in a small room not far from the ship."

"Stay where you are," Luke ordered. "We're right above the ship. We've got the Princess. We'll try to get down to the ship."

Leia looked at the Millennium Falcon in horror. "You came here in that thing!" she gasped. "You're braver than I thought."

Solo didn't know if he'd been insulted or praised. Believing the worst, he gave the Princess a nasty look. "This way," Solo said. "Let's get back to the ship."

Han turned and led the way down the corridor. He hadn't gone very far before he came to an abrupt halt. Twenty armed stormtroopers were marching down the corridor from the other direction!

With lightning speed, Han pulled out his laser pistol and blasted away at the surprised troopers. Solo's first shots dropped two troopers. The others, confused and frightened, turned and ran.

Shouting in several languages, Han chased after the fleeing stormtroopers. Chewie followed his partner more slowly. The explosions and shouts of the battle disappeared down the corridor.

Once again Leia shook her head in wonder at Solo's actions. "Maybe I was wrong," the Princess said. "He certainly has courage!"

"All I know for sure," Luke said, "is that he's an idiot! What good will it do if he gets himself killed? Come on! We can try to get to the ship."

Luke took Leia's hand and they raced toward a corridor that seemed to lead to the Millennium Falcon.

stormtroopers guarding the Millennium Falcon

PREDICTING

Poor Luke and Princess Leia! I don't know what they will do. Oh, Artoo, it is so difficult to PREDICT what people, or even droids, will do.

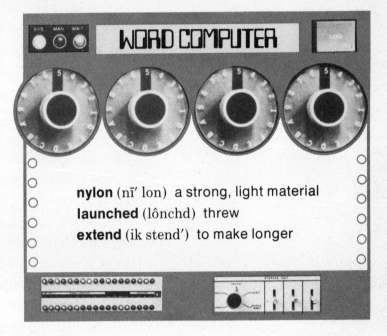

WORD COMPUTER

nylon (nī′ lon) a strong, light material
launched (lônchd) threw
extend (ik stend′) to make longer

TAKEOFF

A good reader can think ahead. He or she will think about what happened in the past to PREDICT what might happen in the FUTURE. PREDICTING FUTURE ACTIONS is almost like drawing conclusions. You have to use the facts that you have.

MISSION

For questions 1, 2, 4, and 5 circle the letter of the choice that best completes each statement. For questions 3 and 6, write your own answers.

1. The stormtroopers will be able to follow Luke and Leia if they ____.
   a. use lasers
   b. get orders to do it
   c. swing across the open pit
   d. cut the tractor beam

2. Luke locked the hatch, hoping the stormtroopers would not be able to ____.
   a. find Han and Chewie
   b. free the Millennium Falcon
   c. help Kenobi
   d. see them

3. Luke and Leia will most likely head for ____.

4. If they had not run away, Luke and Leia would have ____.
   a. been captured
   b. escaped easily
   c. found the plans to the Death Star
   d. found the Millennium Falcon

5. Luke thought he could use the rope to ____.
   a. close the hatch
   b. swing across the trench
   c. extend the bridge
   d. fool the stormtroopers

6. If the rope had not held, Luke and Leia would have ____.

Luke and Leia had not gone far when they were spotted by another patrol of stormtroopers. Luke grabbed Leia's arm and led her down a small hallway. In seconds, the troopers were behind them.

Luke spotted a small hatch. Beyond it was only darkness. "If we could reach that hatch and lock it," Luke thought, "we'd stand a good chance of escaping in the darkness." Luke and Leia ran through the small hatch. They moved quickly onto a dimly lit bridge. Suddenly, the ground beneath Luke's feet was no longer there. If Leia had not grabbed his arm, he would have fallen thousands of feet. For some reason the bridge did not extend over the power trench beneath it.

"Sorry," Luke said. "I think we took a wrong turn."

Laser blasts exploded over their heads. Leia pressed a button on the control panel set into the wall. The hatch behind them closed with a loud thump. Luke drew his laser pistol and shot the control panel, causing the hatch to lock.

"Quick, we've got to get across," Leia said. "Find the controls that extend the bridge to the other side!"

Luke looked unhappily at the still-smoking control panel. "Oh," he said, "I think I just blasted it."

Luke looked around for a way out. From his belt he took a long, thin nylon rope with a hooked end. While Leia covered him with her laser gun, Luke swung the rope over his head, then launched it toward a large overhead pipe. The hook caught the pipe and held fast.

Luke placed his arm about Leia's waist. "We'll swing across!" Luke shouted over the boom of laser blasts.

The Princess reached up and gave a surprised Luke a kiss. "For luck!" she said.

Then, the two swung easily over the power trench and landed safely on the other side. Before the stormtroopers knew what had happened, Luke and Leia disappeared down another corridor.

Luke and Leia swing to safety.

★11 PREDICTING

The story is beginning to frighten me, Artoo. It looks like Kenobi is about to have some trouble with Darth Vader.

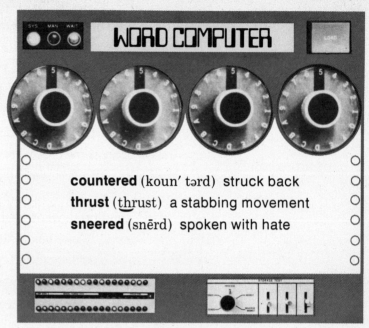

WORD COMPUTER

countered (koun' tərd) struck back
thrust (thrust) a stabbing movement
sneered (snērd) spoken with hate

TAKEOFF

Characters usually act in a certain way. This means you can PREDICT their actions. A good reader will use what is known for a character, plus the FACTS, of the story to make a PREDICTION about what the character will do later in the story.

MISSION

For questions 1 to 4, circle the letter of the choice that best answers each question about the story. For questions 5 and 6, write your own answers.

1. What would Vader do if he found Kenobi's guard down?
   a. make a truce
   b. warn him
   c. try to kill him
   d. capture him

2. What might happen if the battle went on for many hours?
   a. Kenobi's age would help him.
   b. Vader would win out.
   c. Luke would appear.
   d. Han would help Kenobi.

3. What does Kenobi feel will happen if he is struck down?
   a. He will deliver the plans to the Rebels.
   b. He will disappear completely.
   c. He will lead a rebellion.
   d. He will be stronger than ever.

4. When the guards reached the battle what would they most likely do?
   a. ignore the battle
   b. fight among themselves
   c. help Vader
   d. help Kenobi

5. What would Kenobi most like to do in the next few minutes?

   _____

   _____

6. How would Luke react if he saw the battle?

   _____

   _____

Another corridor or two and Kenobi would reach the Millennium Falcon. With all the alarms going off and the talk he had overheard, Kenobi knew that his friends must have rescued the Princess.

All seemed well, yet something bothered him. There was a bad feeling in the air. The Force was not right but what could it be?

Then a huge figure stepped out in front of him, blocking his entry to the hangar not forty feet away. The size and shape of the figure completed the puzzle in Kenobi's mind. His hand moved instantly to his belt.

Darth Vader was the first to speak. "I've been waiting for you, Obi-wan. We meet again, at last. The circle is now complete. When I left you, I was but the learner. Now, I am the master!"

Kenobi countered calmly, "You are only a master of evil, Darth."

The Dark Lord drew his own lightsaber. A hot-pink light was thrust toward Kenobi. The two Jedis, one good and the other evil, moved toward one another. They crossed sabers.

"Your powers are weak, Kenobi," Vader sneered.

Oddly, Kenobi smiled at the Dark Lord. "You can't win, Darth. If you strike me down, I shall become more powerful than you can possibly imagine."

With incredible swiftness, Kenobi moved around Vader and toward the hangar door. For a moment, their sabers met. The two energy fields clashed violently, causing blue and pink sparks to fly.

The crash and thunder of the battle drew the guards away from the Millennium Falcon.

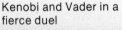
Kenobi and Vader in a fierce duel

⭐ 11 PREDICTING

SOLO

● Do this part of the lesson on your own. Follow the steps that you used in the other parts of the lesson. May the Force be with you!

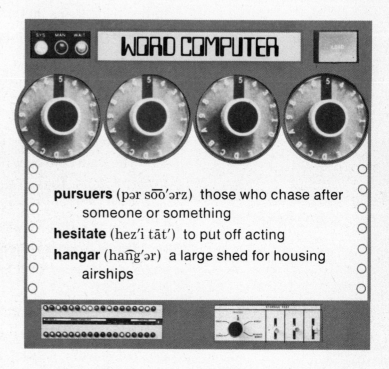

WORD COMPUTER

pursuers (pər sōō′ərz) those who chase after someone or something

hesitate (hez′i tāt′) to put off acting

hangar (haṅg′ər) a large shed for housing airships

MISSION

For questions 1 to 4, circle the letter of the choice that best completes each statement. For questions 5 and 6, write your own answers.

1. The Millennium Falcon will travel ____.
   a. slowly away from the Death Star
   b. to Earth
   c. quickly away from the Death Star
   d. deeper into the Death Star

2. If Luke had not heard Kenobi's voice, he probably would have ____.
   a. been killed
   b. boarded the Millennium Falcon
   c. fought with Kenobi
   d. captured Tarkin

3. In the future Luke will most likely ____.
   a. join the Empire
   b. fight on
   c. return to the farm
   d. capture the Princess

4. If Kenobi had not turned off the tractor beam, the Millennium Falcon would ____.
   a. have brought peace to Alderaan
   b. have destroyed the Death Star
   c. have killed Vader
   d. not have escaped

5. If Kenobi had not slipped aside, he might have ____.

   _____

   _____

6. The Millennium Falcon is probably heading for ____.

   _____

Others were also watching the battle between Kenobi and Vader. Han and Chewie had chased off, then lost, the troopers they had been battling. Luke and Leia had escaped their pursuers. The four met at a large hangar door, and looked across the hangar at the two fighting Jedis.

Han, Luke, Leia, Threepio, Artoo, and Chewbacca meet at the Millennium Falcon.

"Didn't we just leave this party? What kept you?" Solo asked Luke and Leia.

"We ran into some old friends," Leia answered. "Is the ship all right?" she asked Han.

"It seems okay," he said, "if we can get to it. Let's just hope Kenobi knocked out the tractor beam before he started fighting with whomever or whatever that thing is," Han said, pointing toward Vader's huge form.

Kenobi heard the noise of the approaching stormtroopers. He looked up and saw that he was trapped. Taking advantage of Kenobi's lack of attention, Vader brought his laser sword down toward him. Kenobi slipped aside as the laser beam went into the floor.

Kenobi looked directly at Luke for a moment. Then, closing his eyes, he dropped his lightsaber. Vader did not hesitate, and struck Kenobi a mighty blow. The old man appeared to fall, but only his cloak lay on the floor. Vader advanced and poked at the heap of cloth that was once a man. There was no sign of the fallen Jedi. He had completely disappeared.

Luke could not move. He stood and stared at the spot where Ben Kenobi had stood. "Come on! Luke, it's too late!" Leia called.

Then Kenobi's voice came from far away. "Run, Luke! Run!" it commanded.

The sound of Kenobi's voice shocked Luke into action. He fired several laser shots at the charging stormtroopers. Then, he ran up the ramp and into the Millennium Falcon, where the others awaited him. Within seconds, the ship had left the Death Star.

UNIT 12 AUTHOR PURPOSE

Here we are in space again, Artoo. Why must I always suffer? There must be a PURPOSE for my suffering, Artoo. If ever I meet the author of this story, you can be sure I will demand to know why.

WORD COMPUTER

guided (gīd′əd) led
menacing (men′is iñg) threatening
dazed (dāzd) stunned

TAKEOFF

Events in a story happen in a certain sequence. Characters act in particular ways. The author has a PURPOSE for each event and each character.

MISSION

For questions 1 to 4, circle the letter of the choice that best answers each question. For questions 5 and 6, write your own answers.

1. Why did Han whisper a message to his ship?
   a. He was arranging a meeting aboard ship.
   b. He was telling the ship a secret.
   c. He was really afraid she would break up.
   d. He didn't want the Imperial forces to hear.

2. Why does the author say Luke's gun made a menacing hum?
   a. It was about to explode.
   b. It was deadly.
   c. It threatened Luke's life.
   d. It was easy to fire.

3. Why does the author tell you that Leia worked under Chewie's direction?
   a. Leia has never before flown in a starship.
   b. Chewie is smarter than Leia.
   c. A Princess does not fly a starship.
   d. Leia does not know how to fly a starship.

4. Why does Han now call Luke "buddy" and not "kid"?
   a. Luke is now Han's best friend.
   b. He now respects Luke.
   c. Han thinks Luke is young.
   d. Luke has saved the Millennium Falcon.

5. Why did the Princess place her arm about Luke's shoulder?

   _____

   _____

6. Why did Luke not hear the first sounds of the enemy attack?

   _____

   _____

Luke staggered into the cockpit. He barely heard the whine of the energy bolts that bounced off the Millennium Falcon. Leia came over to him and placed her arm about his shoulders.

"There wasn't anything you could have done," she said to Luke.

He looked down sadly. Tears filled Luke's eyes. "I can't believe he's gone. Kenobi and I . . . ''

Han's words and the screams of attacking Imperial TIE fighters interrupted Luke's speech. "Come on, buddy, we're not out of this yet," Han said. Then he guided Luke forward and into the seat of a gun bubble. In front of Luke was a huge laser cannon. Its deadly barrel pointed toward the onrushing TIE fighters.

Luke settled himself into the gunseat and switched on the weapon. A screen lit up and the gun made a menacing hum. Below Luke, Han sat at a similar gun.

Numerous Imperial fighters came at Luke out of the blackness of space. Pressing the trigger, Luke felt the power of the weapon as it split a TIE fighter in two.

Han too fired away at the attacking TIE fighters. Several enemy ships exploded before his eyes.

Without warning, heavy explosions rocked the Millennium Falcon. "We're losing control!" Leia cried out. "Any more hits and we've had it."

Chewbacca strained at the controls of the ship, trying to keep it on course. Leia sat next to him. She pulled and pushed the controls as Chewie directed.

"Don't worry, it will hold together," Han shouted. Several more laser bolts tore into the Millennium Falcon. The old ship rattled and bucked under the new rain of blows. "Hold together," Han whispered to his beloved ship. "Hold together," he pleaded.

All at once, the air aboard the ship grew still. The TIE fighters were gone. They had disappeared as suddenly as they had arrived.

Luke fires at the TIE fighters.

73

Artoo, stop that whistling and chirping. I know you're happy about escaping the Death Star. It was the AUTHOR'S PURPOSE to make your mission quite difficult.

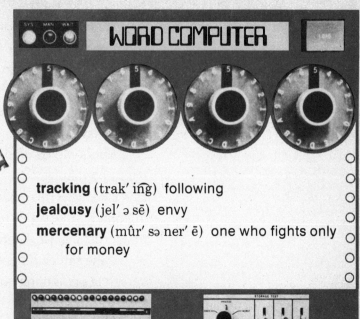

WORD COMPUTER

tracking (trak' ing) following

jealousy (jel' ə sē) envy

mercenary (mûr' sə ner' ē) one who fights only for money

FLIGHT PLAN

An AUTHOR'S PURPOSE is to make a story more enjoyable. This may be done by not telling you everything. The AUTHOR gives you some information, then asks you to make INFERENCES about the story. Understanding the AUTHOR'S PURPOSE helps to make the story more exciting.

MISSION

For questions 1 to 4, circle the letter of the choice that best completes each statement. For questions 5 and 6, write your own answers.

1. Leia is angry with Solo because ____.
   a. he teases Luke too often
   b. the escape was too easy
   c. he fights for money
   d. he does not like her

2. Leia says "This game is not over yet."
   a. she wants to trick Tarkin
   b. she knows the Empire will follow
   c. she fears the Jedis
   d. Kenobi is no longer dangerous

3. Han is trying not to think about the Princess because ____.
   a. he is beginning to like her
   b. she is too rich for him
   c. Luke likes her also
   d. he misses the old Jedi

4. Luke says "I care" to Leia to show that ____.
   a. he wishes to make Han feel ashamed
   b. he believes in the Rebellion
   c. he wants to fool Han
   d. he is teasing Han

5. The Millennium Falcon is being tracked because ____.

   _____

   _____

6. Luke was jealous of Han because ____.

   _____

   _____

"**D**on't get too carried away, Han," the Princess warned. "They let us go! How else would you explain the ease of our escape?"

"Easy! You call that easy?" Han exclaimed. "That was a real rescue, your 'royalness.' A real rescue!"

"They're tracking us" Leia said calmly. "But at least we've got the R-2 unit, and the information seems to be all there."

Han became more interested. "What's so important? What information?"

The Princess answered, "The plans to that battle station we just escaped from. I only hope that a weakness can be found. This little game is not over yet. They plan to follow us back to the Rebel base and then destroy it."

"The game is over for me, sister," Han snapped. "Look, I'm not part of your revolution. And I'm not in it for you, Princess. I expect to be well paid. I'm in it for the money!"

"You needn't worry about your reward. If money is all that you love, then that's what you'll get," Leia said angrily.

Luke and Leia

At that moment, Luke wandered into the cockpit. Leia turned and addressed a startled Luke as if he had been there all the time. "Your friend is quite a mercenary. I wonder if he really cares about anything—or anybody." She then left the cockpit and a totally confused Luke.

"I care," Luke said to the Princess as she closed the door. "What do you think of her, Han?" Luke asked.

"I'm trying not to, kid!" Solo answered. "Still, she's got a lot of spirit. I don't know. What do you think? Do you think a princess and a guy like me could ever . . ." Han let his thoughts trail off.

"No!" Luke snapped.

Han smiled at the younger man's jealousy. Then both men began preparing for the voyage to the Rebel base.

SOLO ● Do this part of the lesson on your own. Follow the steps you used in the other parts of the lesson. May the Force be with you!

WORD COMPUTER

drifted (drift′ əd) flew slowly
temple (tem′ pəl) house of worship
proton torpedo (prō′ ton tôr pē′ dō) a deadly bomb

MISSION For questions 1 to 4, circle the letter of the choice that best answers each question. For questions 5 and 6, write your own answers.

1. Why does the author have the young pilot say "Impossible"?
   a. to show it is impossible
   b. to show he is not a good pilot
   c. to show the task is difficult
   d. to show that Rebels are poor pilots

2. Why was Artoo chirping at great speed?
   a. He is quite angry.
   b. He is about to complete his mission.
   c. He wants to make Threepio jealous.
   d. He likes being carried.

3. Why were some Rebel ships made of scraps?
   a. The ships were powerful.
   b. The ships had no weapons.
   c. The ships were weak.
   d. The Rebels weren't wasteful.

4. Why does the author say that the temple is huge?
   a. It houses the entire Rebel spacefleet.
   b. It was once a temple.
   c. The Force is with the Rebels.
   d. The Millennium Falcon is battered.

5. Why did General Dodonna seem not to hear the young pilot's words?

   _____

   _____

6. Where is the Rebel base located?

   _____

   _____

Many hours later, the battered Millennium Falcon drifted over the Fourth Moon of Yavin. It was here that the Rebel base was located.

At Leia's direction, Han guided the small starship through the doors of what had once been a huge temple. It was now the hidden fortress of the Rebel army.

The Millennium Falcon landed in a giant hangar. In it were the entire Rebel spacefleet. The ships were old but well cared for. Some seemed to be built from metal scraps.

The Millennium Falcon was met by Commander Willard, leader of the Rebel forces. He rushed to Leia and hugged her. Then he stepped back and bowed. "When we heard about Alderaan, we feared the worst."

"There is no time for sorrow, Commander," the Princess said. "Take the R-2 unit aboard this ship and use the information in it to plan our attack against the Death Star. Hurry! It is our only hope!"

Two Rebel soldiers carried Artoo away. He was chirping at a very great speed.

That evening, a grim General Dodonna addressed a small group of Rebel pilots and their R-2 assistance units. "Princess Leia has brought us the plans to the battle station. We have studied them and there is a weakness.

General Dodonna greets Leia.

"The battle station is heavily protected. It carries more firepower than half the Imperial starfleet. But its defenses are built to stop attacks by land-based laser cannons and large starships. A small one-pilot fighter should be able to get past the defenses and fire a proton torpedo into an open exhaust port."

Wedge Antilles, a young pilot, spoke out. "Impossible!" he shouted. "Even with a computer it's impossible. That port is less than six feet wide."

"It's not impossible," Luke answered. "I used to shoot womp rats back home. Womp rats aren't much bigger than two meters.

General Dodonna seemed not to hear the young pilot. "Man your ships," he ordered. Then he said, "May the Force be with you!"

SOLO

● In this Unit you are going to practice the reading skills that you have learned in Units 1-12. Think about each question before you answer it.

Artoo, I do hope Luke takes care of himself. He is such a good person. He does look rather fine in that pilot's uniform. Yes, Artoo, you look very fine too.

WORD COMPUTER

beat up (bēt up) worn out
date (dāt) a meeting
boring (bôr′ ĭng) tiresome

MISSION

For questions 1 to 4, circle the letter of the choice that best completes each sentence about the story. For questions 5 and 6, write your own answers.

1. The best title for this story is ____.
   a. Old Debts
   b. Luke's Dream
   c. The X- wing Fighter
   d. The Takeoff

2. You can tell from Luke's words that the Rebels ____.
   a. are greatly outnumbered
   b. will lose the battle
   c. outnumber Imperial forces
   d. will not fight well

3. The choice that is a fact is ____.
   a. Luke felt Han would stay on
   b. Luke thought his fighter was swift
   c. the driver thought Artoo was ''beat up''
   d. Han has debts

4. The first thing that happened in the story was ____.
   a. Han loaded the Millennium Falcon
   b. Luke left the meeting hall
   c. Han left the meeting hall
   d. Leia flew an X-Wing fighter

5. In the story, the word ''lifted'' means ____.

   _____

   _____

6. Han's and Chewie's leaving caused Luke to be ____.

   _____

   _____

Luke, Threepio, and Artoo left the meeting hall. The hangar before them was filled with Rebel fighters. Each tiny fighter stood armed and ready for its mission.

Han and Chewie stood to one side of the hangar. They were loading small boxes aboard the Millennium Falcon. The sight of his friends preparing to leave saddened Luke. He had thought they might stay on and help in the fight to come. "So, you got your reward and now you're leaving!" Luke said angrily.

Han nodded. "I've got some old debts to pay off. Even if I didn't, you don't think I'd be fool enough to stick around here? Why don't you come with us? You're pretty good in a fight. We could use you."

"Come on, Han," Luke said. "Look around! You know what's about to happen and what we're up against. You're turning your back on us."

Solo looked at Luke. "What good is a reward if you're not around to spend it?"

"Take care of yourself, Han," Luke said quietly. "But I guess that's what you're best at, isn't it?" Luke walked to the other side of the hangar.

Han and Chewbacca prepare to leave.

Luke reached the small X-wing fighter he was to fly and climbed in. A truck pulled up to Luke's ship. Artoo sat in back. The truck's driver called up to Luke in the cockpit of the X-wing fighter. "This R-2 unit of yours seems a bit beat up. Do you want a new one?"

"Not on your life!" Luke said with certainty. "That little droid and I have been through a lot together."

Threepio looked worriedly up toward the X-wing fighter's cockpit as Artoo was gently placed in a position behind Luke. "Hang on, Artoo. You've got to come back. You wouldn't want my life to get boring, would you?"

Luke moved the swift little fighter along the runway and into the air. As the tiny ship lifted off, Luke heard a voice he thought he would never hear again. "Be strong, Luke," Kenobi's voice whispered. "The Force will be with you."

Did you know, Artoo, that I myself had a chance to attend Pilot School? However, my calling was closer to the ground. I hope I have done some good down here!

WORD COMPUTER

metallic (mə tal′ik) relating to metal
chatter (chat′ər) small talk
accelerate (ak sel′ə rāt′) to increase speed
exhaust (ig zôst′) escape of steam or gases from an engine

MISSION For questions 1 to 4, circle the letter of the choice that best answers each question. For questions 5 and 6, write your own answers.

1. What caused the fire on the Death Star?
   a. Antilles' chatter
   b. Biggs's reply
   c. Luke's torpedo
   d. the Death Star's cannons

2. What can you tell about Wedge Antilles?
   a. He is a better pilot than Biggs.
   b. He is a better pilot than Luke.
   c. He likes to talk.
   d. He has never been in battle.

3. Where is the exhaust port located?
   a. in a trench
   b. in the meeting hall
   c. in an X-wing fighter
   d. in a wall speaker

4. Which would best describe Luke's attitude?
   a. afraid of Biggs
   b. sure of himself
   c. angry with Biggs
   d. unhappy with his X-wing fighter

5. Why hadn't Luke seen Biggs before this?

   _____

   _____

6. In the story, what does the word ''rate'' mean?

   _____

   _____

Princess Leia, General Dodonna, and Threepio stood looking at a large circular viewscreen. It showed the planet Yavin and her four moons. A moving red dot showed the approach of the Death Star toward Yavin and its moons.

A loud metallic voice came through a wall speaker. "Our ships are away and on course. The Death Star is nearing us at a rate that will bring us within its firing range in fifteen minutes.

Several squadrons of X- and Y-wing fighters formed miles high in space. They searched ahead for the Death Star. Wedge Antilles, the young pilot Luke had met earlier, was the first to see the Imperial battle station. "Look at the size of that thing!" he cried out.

"Cut the chatter, Antilles!" the leader of Red Squadron ordered. "Accelerate to attack speed. This is it boys. Hit it!"

Luke dove toward the Death Star with the other members of Red Squadron. Their X-wing fighters twisted and turned as they made their screaming dive. A storm of laser fire rose upward from the Death Star.

The battle station grew larger and larger in Luke's sights. Energy bolts and laser beams thundered from the weapons of Luke's fighter. One started a huge fire on the Death Star's surface.

"I got it," Luke cried out happily. But his joy turned quickly to terror. At the speed he was traveling, Luke couldn't help but pass through the very fire he had started.

"Pull out, Luke! Pull out!" called the voice of Red Leader. It was no use. Luke's X-wing fighter shot into a wall of flame.

The voice of an old friend reached Luke in his cockpit. "Luke, this is Biggs. I just got here from another base. I didn't want to miss any of the fun. Are you all right?"

"Biggs! Biggs, old buddy." Luke said. "I got a little cooked, but I'm all right. Let's find the exhaust port in that trench."

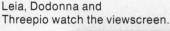

Leia, Dodonna and Threepio watch the viewscreen.

REVIEW 13

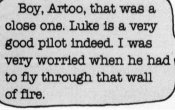

Boy, Artoo, that was a close one. Luke is a very good pilot indeed. I was very worried when he had to fly through that wall of fire.

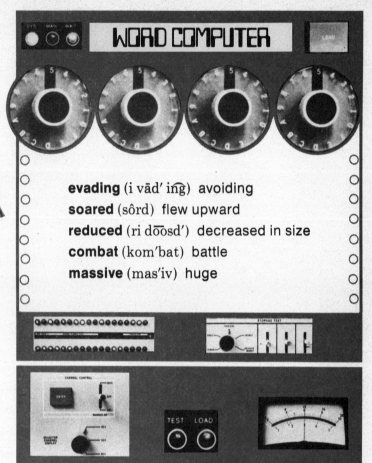

WORD COMPUTER

evading (i vād′ iṅg) avoiding
soared (sôrd) flew upward
reduced (ri d o͞o sd′) decreased in size
combat (kom′bat) battle
massive (mas′iv) huge

MISSION

For questions 1 to 4, circle the letter of the choice that best completes each sentence about the story. For questions 5 and 6, write your own answers.

1. The main idea of this story is that ____.
   a. TIE fighters fly in formation.
   b. Luke is almost killed
   c. the Rebel pilots are in danger
   d. Darth Vader has a personal ship

2. The choice that is an opinion is ____.
   a. thirty Rebel ships were counted
   b. Wedge was a good shot
   c. a TIE fighter was destroyed
   d. an energy bolt hit Luke's ship

3. You can tell from the story that ____.
   a. Wedge was nearly shot down
   b. Vader had already shot down several Rebel ships
   c. Some Rebel ships had been shot down
   d. Luke fired at Vader

4. The author tells you that Luke may have spoken too soon because ____.
   a. Vader is coming
   b. Luke talks too much
   c. Wedge did not hear him
   d. the Rebel attack caused problems

5. You can tell that the Death Star's cannon cannot hit ____.

   _____

   _____

6. In the story, the word "hurtled" means ____.

   _____

   _____

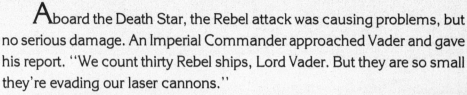

Aboard the Death Star, the Rebel attack was causing problems, but no serious damage. An Imperial Commander approached Vader and gave his report. "We count thirty Rebel ships, Lord Vader. But they are so small they're evading our laser cannons."

Vader nodded. "We'll have to destroy them ship to ship. Commander, get the crews to their fighters. And prepare my personal ship for combat."

Luke, Biggs, and Wedge Antilles soared high above the Death Star. Luke spotted the trench where the exhaust port was hidden. He signalled his find to his two wingmen, and the three X-wing fighters dove down and into the massive trench. Imperial laser cannons shot deadly energy bolts at the fighters as they hurtled toward their target.

Below him, Luke could see the still-smoking remains of Rebel ships and pilots whose luck had run out. Luke's thoughts were pulled back to his own safety by the crash of an energy bolt that nearly tore his ship apart.

"Watch it, Luke," warned Wedge. "There's a TIE fighter on your back."

Somehow, Wedge managed to slip behind the TIE fighter. A touch of the firing button on Wedge's control panel reduced the TIE fighter to a puff of fire and smoke.

"Good shooting, Wedge," Luke called out. "We should be able to make a complete attack run now."

But Luke may have spoken too soon. Darth Vader was already setting his firing control buttons as his TIE fighter dropped like a stone toward Luke and his friends.

"Stay in attack formation!" commanded the Sith Lord to his two wingmen. "I'll take those ships myself."

SOLO

In this Unit you are going to pratice the reading skills that you have learned in Units 1-12. Think about each question before you answer it.

WORD COMPUTER

wiped out (wīpd' out') destroyed

squadron (skwod' rən) a group of starships

rose (rōz) stood up

MISSION   For questions 1 to 4, circle the letter of the choice that best answers each question. For questions 5 and 6, write your own answers.

1. Why was Leia listening with more than normal interest?
   a. Artoo is in danger.
   b. Luke is now a Rebel.
   c. She likes Luke a great deal.
   d. Han has left.

2. What did Luke most likely do in Beggar's Canyon?
   a. look for Leia
   b. hunt stormtroopers
   c. meet Biggs
   d. fly X-wing fighters

3. What can you infer about Yavin?
   a. It has no moons.
   b. It has no life on it.
   c. It has only one moon.
   d. It has at least three other moons.

4. What conclusion can you draw about the Rebel forces?
   a. They have almost destroyed the Death Star.
   b. They have lost many pilots.
   c. They will soon retreat.
   d. They will soon land on the Death Star.

5. What was the last thing the three pilots did?

   _____

   _____

6. How does Luke hope to fend off the TIE fighters?

   _____

   _____

On the Fourth Moon of Yavin, Princess Leia Organa rose from her chair. She bent to check the viewscreen. She studied it for a moment, then shook her head. The Death Star was coming nearer.

"Can our attack go on?" Leia asked General Dodonna.

"It must," the General replied.

"But we've lost so many ships and pilots already," the Princess said. "Blue Squadron is all but wiped out. And Red Squadron has only a few ships in the air."

"Our only hope is Red Squadron," Dodonna said, pointing to the viewscreen. "Look, there goes your young friend, Luke and his two wingmen. They seem to have located the trench."

The sound of Luke's voice came over the radio. Leia listened with more than normal interest. "Close it up, Wedge," Luke ordered. "Biggs, where are you?" Luke asked.

"Over here, boss," came Biggs' answer.

Satisfied that his two wingmen were with him, Luke began his run on the target. "Biggs, Wedge, let's close it up. We're going in at full power. That ought to keep any TIE fighters off our backs."

"Luke, at that speed will you be able to pull up in time?" Biggs asked with worry in his voice.

"It'll be just like Beggar's Canyon back home, Biggs," Luke said.

The three tiny fighters rocketed down the trench at attack speed. Their target lay ahead.

Luke and Wedge battle the TIE fighters.

Look, Artoo, there goes Darth Vader again. You'll have to excuse me, Artoo. I must go to work now. Yes, he's the one who shot you. I may have to take care of that evil fellow myself.

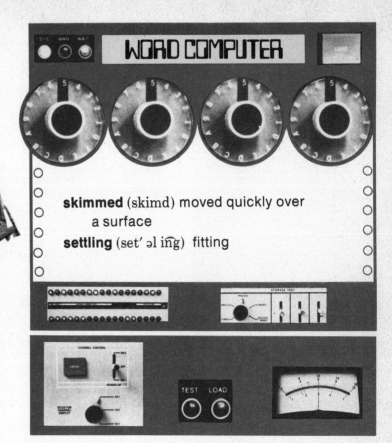

WORD COMPUTER

skimmed (skimd) moved quickly over a surface

settling (set' əl iṅg) fitting

MISSION

For questions 1 to 4, circle the letter of the choice that best completes each sentence about the story. For questions 5 and 6, write your own answers.

1. The main idea of the story is that ____.
   a. Biggs has flown away
   b. Kenobi is flying an X-wing fighter
   c. Luke feels the Force
   d. Luke is alone

2. A name that Vader uses to refer to Luke is
   ____.
   a. the farmer
   b. the leader
   c. the young Jedi
   d. the older man

3. A word that could describe Biggs is ____.
   a. calm
   b. witty
   c. excitable
   d. angry

4. The number of TIE fighters that first appeared was ____.
   a. six
   b. two
   c. four
   d. three

5. The voice that told Luke to use the Force belonged to ____.

   _____

   _____

6. Wedge was unable to see ____.

   _____

   _____

As Luke, Wedge, and Biggs skimmed over the trench, three TIE fighters followed at a distance.

Wedge's worried voice came over Luke's radio. "My computer screen shows the trench, but I can't see the exhaust port! Are you sure the computer can hit it, Luke?"

"TIE fighters are on our backs," Biggs calmly reported.

"Biggs, you and Wedge take care of those fighters. I'll worry about the exhaust port," Luke ordered.

Biggs gunned his X-wing fighter up and away from the trench. Wedge did the same, but went in another direction. A TIE fighter took off after each ship. Vader alone remained to stop Luke.

"Stay with those other two," Vader ordered his wingmen. "I'm staying with the leader." Vader tried settling Luke into his gun sights, but was unable to do so. "The Force is strong with this one," Vader thought.

As Luke moved to set up his own targeting computer a strange feeling came over him. A voice, the voice of Ben Kenobi, filled his cockpit. "Use the Force, Luke," Kenobi said. "Let go, Luke. Trust me. Trust the Force."

Luke obeyed Kenobi's words. He switched off his targeting computer. A new look came over his face. Luke knew he could use the Force to guide his proton torpedoes to their target. He was never so sure of anything in his life. Luke knew the Force would be with him.

I certainly am glad that Luke remembered to use the Force. I am sure that he will be able to destroy the Death Star with those torpedoes.

WORD COMPUTER

reaches (rēch′ əz) area
catapulted (kat′ə pult′ əd)
ecstatic (ek stat′ ik) very happy

MISSION   For questions 1 to 4, circle the letter of the choice that best answers each question. For questions 5 and 6, write your own answers.

1. In the story, what does the word "trench" mean?
   a. area
   b. road
   c. pit
   d. field

2. What is the best title for this story?
   a. Han's Return
   b. The Millennium Falcon
   c. A Confused General
   d. Vader's Victim

3. What conclusion can you draw from Dodonna's actions?
   a. Dodonna does not know about the Force.
   b. Luke is not acting normally.
   c. He is angry with Luke.
   d. He does not like Leia

4. What was the cause of Vader's spinning off into hyperspace?
   a. Han's laser cannon
   b. Luke's proton torpedoes
   c. poor steering
   d. a solar storm

5. What would most likely have happened if Han had not showed up?

   _____

   _____

6. What was the effect of Luke's hearing Han's voice?

   _____

   _____

At the Rebel base, a confused General Dodonna spoke into a radio. "Luke, your targeting computer is off. What's wrong?"

"Nothing," Luke answered. "I'm all right!"

"But Luke," Dodonna continued, "without your targeting computer you'll never be able to . . ."

The sound of the General's voice was drowned out by the roar of explosions. Laserfire from Vader's cannons had struck Luke's ship. Smoke and sparks poured out of Artoo. The little droid had been hit.

"I've lost Artoo," Luke reported.

In the control room, Threepio called out to his friend. "Artoo! Oh, no. Hang on, old friend!" the golden droid begged.

Behind Luke, the evil Vader was preparing to fire his cannons once again. "I have you now," Vader hissed, as his finger moved toward the firing button.

Without warning, the Dark Lord's ship was rocked by powerful laser blasts. Both he and his ship were actually catapulted from the trench by the force of the explosions. In seconds, the TIE fighter and its pilot were spinning helplessly through space. Completely out of control, Darth Vader disappeared into the endless reaches of hyperspace.

In the cockpit of the Millennium Falcon, Han Solo and Chewbacca were grinning from ear to ear. Han's ecstatic voice came over Luke's radio. "You're all clear, kid. Now let's blow this thing and go home."

Luke looked up at the Millennium Falcon as it flew high over the Death Star. He smiled, then continued his attack run. Nothing could stop him now!

laser bursts in the trench

SOLO

● In this Unit you are going to practice the reading skills that you have learned in Units 1-12. Think about each question before you answer it.

This is it, Artoo. What? You say you missed this part? I know, Artoo. You were hurt, my little friend. You must read all about Luke. He was wonderful.

WORD COMPUTER

standing by (stan′dĭng bī) ready
evacuate (ĭ vak′ yōō āt′) to leave

MISSION

For questions 1 to 4, circle the letter of the choice that best completes each sentence about the story. For questions 5 and 6, write your own answers.

1. The main idea of the story is that ____.
   a. the Death Star has been destroyed
   b. Luke has survived
   c. Tarkin is dead
   d. Han is happy

2. The Death Star would burn for many ____.
   a. days
   b. weeks
   c. hours
   d. minutes

3. The choice that has nothing to do with the last moments of the Death Star is ____.
   a. burning pieces
   b. a mighty wind
   c. a bright flash
   d. a personal starship

4. In the story, the word "flowing" means ____.
   a. hurting
   b. flowering
   c. passing through
   d. rocking

5. The last person to speak to Luke was ____.

   _____

   _____

6. You can tell Tarkin thinks the Death Star is safe because ____.

   _____

   _____

90

In the control room of the Imperial battle station, Governor Tarkin watched the Rebel attack with interest. An Imperial Commander stood nearby.

"Governor Tarkin, we have studied their attack plan and there is a danger. Shall I have your personal starship standing by?"

Tarkin grinned evilly. "Would you have me evacuate in our moment of victory? I think you give these Rebels too much credit. We shall press on with our attack. The Rebel base, and the entire moon for that matter, will meet the same fate as Alderaan."

Tarkin turned to watch the huge viewscreen over his desk. This was one show he did not want to miss.

Unknown to Tarkin, Luke's X-wing fighter carrying a load of deadly proton torpedoes was nearing its target. Luke felt the power of the Force flowing through his body. His hands rested lightly on the firing control buttons of his fighter.

Without thinking, Luke's fingers pressed the buttons. The X-wing fighters rocked slightly as the proton torpedoes began their run. Both torpedoes entered the tiny exhaust port as if they had eyes to guide them.

Luke pulled up quickly and began a steep climb. Seconds later, the tiny ship was given a push upward by what seemed to be a mighty wind. Then a flash as bright as an exploding sun lit the sky.

The Death Star had blown up and its flaming remains would burn for days over the planet Yavin.

"Good shot, kid. That was one in a million!" Han cheered.

Luke could not help but grin. Kenobi's voice came to him again. "Remember that the Force will be with you . . . always."

Luke, and what was left of the Rebel spacefleet, headed back toward their base. The group was led by an old space freighter named the Millennium Falcon.

The Death Star explodes.

Artoo, I insist you read this part of the story. You will see how brave I was. Why, I did a lot to try and help you. Why, thank you, Artoo. I know you would do the same for me.

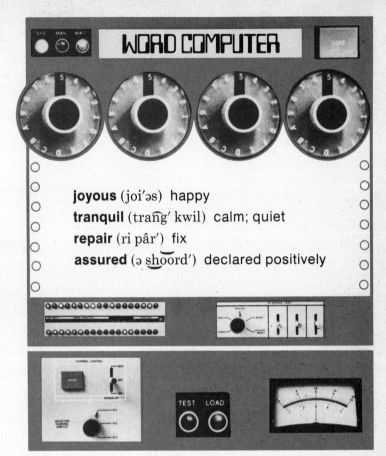

WORD COMPUTER

joyous (joi′əs) happy
tranquil (trang′ kwil) calm; quiet
repair (ri pâr′) fix
assured (ə shoord′) declared positively

MISSION

For questions 1 to 4, circle the letter of the choice that best answers each question. For questions 5 and 6, write your own answers.

1. Which of the following statements is **not** a fact?
   a. Leia threw her arms around Luke.
   b. Artoo was badly burned.
   c. Luke believed Artoo would be fine.
   d. Two soldiers lifted Artoo from the cockpit.

2. What does the author tell you about See Threepio?
   a. He is afraid of Vader.
   b. He cares for Artoo.
   c. He does not care for Artoo.
   d. He would like an oil bath.

3. Which statement tells about Leia?
   a. She never gave up on Han.
   b. She does not stick by her friends.
   c. She is a better pilot than Luke.
   d. She does not like crowds.

4. In the story, what does the word "reunion" mean?
   a. a new union.
   b. an organization
   c. a meeting after a separation
   d. a gathering for dinner

5. What is the main idea in this part of the story?

   _____

   _____

6. What was the cause of the Rebels' joy?

   _____

   _____

A cheering mob met the returning Rebel ships. Each fighter was surrounded by happy people.

Luke's ship was more tranquil. Princess Leia, General Dodonna, Commander Willard, and several other Rebel officers lined up to congratulate Luke.

When the others had left, Leia threw her arms around Luke. They hugged and danced in circles until both were too tired to go on.

In a few moments, Han and Chewie joined them. The four friends had a joyous reunion. Luke looked at Han. "I knew you'd come back, Han," he said. "I just knew it."

Solo grinned. "Well, I wasn't going to let you get all the credit and take all the reward, was I?"

Leia laughed. "Hey, I knew there was more to you than money," she said to Solo.

Luke suddenly looked worried. Two soldiers were lifting Artoo down from the fighter's cockpit. A worried Threepio stood to the side watching. The little droid had been badly burned. Pieces of wiring and broken tubes could be seen in the droid's body.

"You can repair him, can't you?" Threepio asked. "Oh, my! Artoo! Can you hear me? Say something," Threepio cried out.

"You must repair him," Threepio said to Luke. "Sir, if any of my body parts will help, you may certainly take them."

"We'll get to work on him right away," one of the soldiers said to Threepio.

"I believe Artoo is going to be fine," Luke assured the tall droid at his side. Threepio nodded. For once, he had nothing to say.

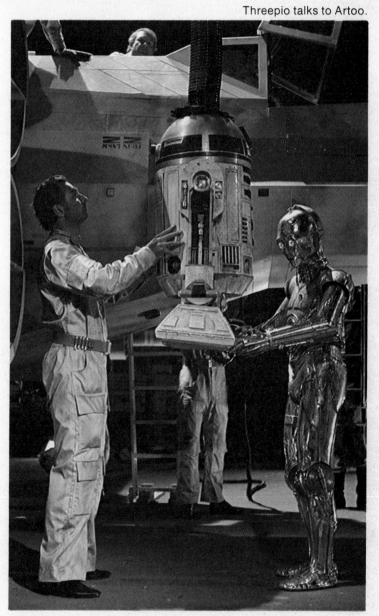

Threepio talks to Artoo.

⭐15 REVIEW

Oh, my poor little friend. You have been so badly hurt. But Luke says you are going to be fine. I hope that we will stay friends forever, Artoo.

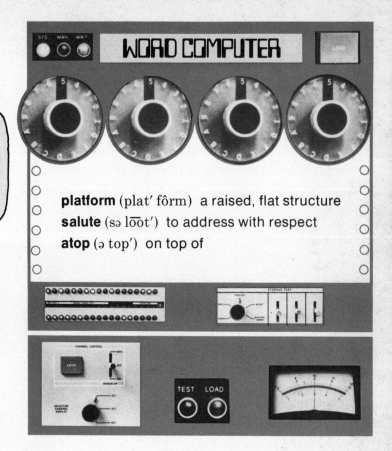

WORD COMPUTER

platform (plat' fôrm) a raised, flat structure
salute (sə lo͞ot') to address with respect
atop (ə top') on top of

MISSION

For questions 1 to 4, circle the letter of the choice that best completes each sentence about the story. For questions 5 and 6, write your own answers.

1. Chewbacca did not receive a medal _____.
   a. he already had one
   b. he did not want it
   c. he was nervous in crowds
   d. he did not deserve one

2. You can infer that _____.
   a. Luke and Han will continue to fight against the Empire
   b. Tarkin has escaped
   c. the Rebels would now live in peace
   d. Dodonna was the only Rebel general

3. The character who roared his happiness was _____.
   a. Kenobi
   b. See Threepio
   c. Chewbacca
   d. Han Solo

4. You can conclude that Artoo _____.
   a. could not be fixed
   b. was as good as new
   c. was not happy
   d. was angry with Threepio

5. A good title for this part of the story might be _____.

   _____

   _____

6. When the author writes "They knew the applause was not for them," he means _____.

   _____

   _____

The giant room that had once been a temple was filled for the first time in thousands of years. Hundreds of Rebel pilots, officers, soldiers, and their families stood at attention.

They had come from all over the galaxy. They were here to honor those who had fought to free the galaxy from the evil Imperial battle station known as the Death Star.

At the far end of the room, Princess Leia stood on a high marble platform. Behind her stood the leaders of the Rebel forces.

Two large wooden doors faced the Princess at the other end of the temple. They opened slowly and Han Solo, Luke Skywalker, and Chewbacca entered the enormous room. The crowd turned to salute them. Luke and Han were clearly enjoying the attention, but Chewbacca roared his happiness.

A newly rebuilt and polished Artoo Detoo stood to one side of the platform. Next to him stood See Threepio, his faithful friend. Both droids could barely stand still. The excitement was too much for them. Artoo's whistles, chirps, and beeps told of his happiness.

Luke, Chewie, and Han climbed the steps to the platform and stood before the Princess. Leia placed a large, golden medal about the neck of each man. Chewbacca would receive his medal later at a quieter moment.

When the ceremony was complete the hundreds of rebels who had gathered there applauded with happiness.

Princess Leia, Luke, Han, Chewbacca, Artoo, and Threepio stood together atop the platform. They raised their arms and smiled. They knew that the applause was not for them but for the newly gained freedom in their part of the galaxy. The Rebels looked forward to the day when the entire galaxy would be free.

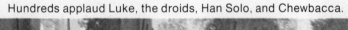
Hundreds applaud Luke, the droids, Han Solo, and Chewbacca.

Answer Key

Unit 1
(p. 6)   1. c   2. b   3. d   4. c   5. a tall, rocky rise
6. Mos Eisley spaceport

(p. 8)   1. c   2. d   3. a   4. b   5. a laser gun
6. 3 or 4 seasons

(p. 10)   1. c   2. b   3. d   4. a   5. laughter and fighting
6. the weak-minded

Unit 2
(p. 12)   1. c   2. a   3. a   4. a   5. bright yellow; toothy
6. one; thousand; no

(p. 14)   1. c   2. d   3. b   4. a   5. The Monster
6. a laser pistol

(p. 16)   1. b   2. c   3. d   4. c   5. Kenobi Kills the
Monster   6. a split-second

Unit 3
(p. 18)   1. c   2. b, c, e, g,   3. Kenobi and Solo Make
a Deal   4. in a dark corner

(p. 20)   1. Solo accepts Kenobi's offer.   2. a, d, f, h, i
3. The Deal Is Closed   4. seventeen thousand

(p. 22)   1. Solo owes money to Jabba.   2. a. Han needs
the seventeen thousand   b. Han is in danger
c. There is a price on Solo's head.
d. Jabba might take Solo's ship.   e. Han kills
Greedo.   3. Solo Makes a Deal   4. Jabba

Unit 4
(p. 24)   1. c   2. b   3. d   4. a   5. a bit; a break or split
6. be careful; look at

(p. 26)   1. c   2. a   3. b   4. d   5. strength   6. brags

(p. 28)   1. c   2. d   3. b   4. a   5. small   6. large

Unit 5
(p. 30)   1. d   2. a   3. a   4. d   5. It began to rise.
6. He fired back.

(p. 32)   1. c   2. d   3. a   4. b   5. The ship lost a
deflector shield.   6. A red light flashed.

(p. 34)   1. c   2. d   3. b   4. b   5. Kenobi fell back.
6. pull someone's arms off

Unit 6
(p. 36)   1. c   2. b   3. d   4. c   5. break apart
6. puzzled

(p. 38)   1. c   2. a   3. d   4. b   5. the Empire
6. It rocketed forward.

(p. 40)   1. c   2. a   3. d   4. b   5. It got lost or was
part of a convoy.   6. It pulled the ship in.

Unit 7
(p. 42)   1. c   2. a   3. c   4. a   5. He remembered
something bad.   6. He snapped to attention.

(p. 44)   1. c   2. d   3. b   4. d   5. lifted the two droids
6. to disguise themselves; to go deeper
into the Death Star

(p. 46)   1. b   2. b   3. a   4. d   5. wise, kind, great
6. upset

Unit 8
(p. 48)   1. c   2. b   3. d   4. a   5. He wants to save
Leia.   6. pay him

(p. 50)   1. c   2. b   3. a   4. c   5. Stormtroopers
are coming.   6. Luke and Han would have
been caught.

(p. 52)   1. a   2. a   3. c   4. d   5. gone
6. a combination of fear and respect

Unit 9
(p. 54)   1. a   2. b   3. d   4. c   5. easy   6. to get into
the garbage chute

(p. 56)   1. c   2. c   3. a   4. d   5. The walls will come
together.   6. They will be killed.

(p. 58)   1. b   2. a   3. c   4. b   5. The walls would
have come together.   6. Their lives had
been saved.

Unit 10
(p. 60)   1. O   2. F   3. F   4. O   5. F   6. F
(p. 62)   1. O   2. F   3. O   4. F   5. O   6. F
(p. 64)   1. F   2. F   3. F   4. O   5. F   6. O
7. O   8. F

Unit 11
(p. 66)   1. c   2. d   3. The Milennium Falcon
4. a   5. b   6. fallen into the trench

(p. 68)   1. c   2. b   3. d   4. c   5. overcome Vader
6. He would be upset.

(p. 70)   1. c   2. a   3. b   4. d   5. been hit
6. The Rebel base

Unit 12
(p. 72)   1. c   2. a   3. d   4. b   5. to make him feel
better   6. He was too upset about Kenobi.

(p. 74)   1. c   2. b   3. a   4. b   5. They have the R-2
unit.   6. Han is interested in The Princess.

(p. 76)   1. c   2. b   3. d   4. a   5. He is worried.
6. over the Fourth Moon of Yavin